CARA MIA

The
David Whitfield
Story

Alan Britton

Highgate Publications (Beverley) Ltd
1993

i

David Whitfield had a great love for his home town, Hull, and his name has been commemorated in the City in a number of ways: among them David Whitfield Close, the David Whitfield Rose Garden, the David Whitfield Baby Unit, and a plaque and bust in the New Theatre.

British Library Cataloguing in Publication Data
Britton, Alan Michael
   Cara Mia: David Whitfield Story
   I. Title
      782.42164092

ISBN 0-948929-86-3

© 1994 Alan Michael Britton

ISBN 0 948929 86 3

Published by
Highgate Publications (Beverley) Ltd.
24 Wylies Road, Beverley, HU17 7AP
Telephone (0482) 866826

Produced by

4 Newbegin, Lairgate, Beverley, HU17 8EG
Telephone (0482) 886017

Cover picture of David Whitfield: Courtesy Deram Group Records Archive

Contents

Acknowledgements

The author would like to express his appreciation to members of the Whitfield family who were most helpful and supportive in the writing of this book and also to Mr. Bill Wilkins for the time spent in research, without which the book could not have been written. He extends his sincere gratitude to all who have so generously helped and co-operated with him and in particular:

Mrs. Shiela Whitfield; Mr. Lance Whitfield; Mr. Keith Whitfield; Mrs. Lily Smith (née Whitfield); Mr. Ted Whitfield; Mr. and Mrs. Walter (née Doris Whitfield); *The News* (Portsmouth); *Navy News*; BBC Radio Humberside; *Hull Daily Mail*; *The Guinness Book of British Hit Singles*; *Melody Maker*; *The Universe*; Local Studies Library, Hull Central Library; Polygram International Ltd.; Deram Group Records Archives; Mr. Bill Wilkins; David Whitfield Appreciation Society; Mr. Vernon Brand; Mr. Bruce Palmer; David Whitfield Commemorative Society; The Friends of The Imperial War Museum; The *Ramillies* Association; The *Black Swan* Association; Mr. John Solway, The Imperial War Museum; Gandy's Roses Ltd.; Mr. Hughie Green; Mr. Ronnie Hilton: Mr. Bert Gaunt; Mr. Reg Williams; Mr. Brian Goddard, The Grand Theatre, Wolverhampton; Mr. Ted Bates, J.P. (Australia); Mr. C. W. Bourner; Mrs. Pearl Bentley; Mrs. Janet Barringer; Mr. H. Brocklehurst; Mrs. Joan Clash (Australia); Mrs. Elizabeth Collis; Mr. Ken Cochrane; Mr. Peter Cawley (U.S.A.); Mrs. Dannett: Mrs. W. Evans; Mr. Bill Gawthorpe; Mrs. E. Hollome; Mrs. Jean Kelly; Mr. Ken Mountjoy; Mr. H. McCracken; Mrs. Doreen Nash; Mr. Clarry Owen; Mr. D. H. Powell; Mr. Derrick Prigg; Mr. Ronnie Porte; Mr. George Roberts; Mrs. Norah Roantree; Mrs. Dorothy Smith; Mrs. Annette Sellick; Mrs. G. E. Sorrell; Mr. Malcolm Steer; Mr. Derek Thompson; Mr. Norman Walker; Mrs. Eileen Ward; Mr. Gordon White (Australia); Innes Studios, Hessle.

The photograph of *H.M.S. Sirius* is British Crown Copyright Reserved and is reproduced by special permission.

Publisher's Note

The originals of some of the early photographs of David Whitfield and his family are of poor quality but are included because of their unique interest.

Chapter One

The Final Return

It was a mid-February day in 1980 when the frigate, *H.M.S. Sirius*, slipped away from its Hull-side berth and headed out down the Humber, towards the open sea, carrying the remains of one of Hull's most famous sons. The casket of his ashes had travelled halfway across the world, from the heat of an Australian summer to the cold of a northern English winter.

February is usually a vile month on this stretch of the North Sea coast, with the wind howling from the Arctic and piercing down the Humber like a knife. But this particular day, although overcast and grey, was comparatively mild. Having lived and known the peculiarities of this stretch of coast for most of his life, he would have recognised the unseasonal calm straight away. The sea was unusually placid as the sleek grey vessel left the shelter of the estuary. It passed the narrow ribbon of causeway leading to Spurn Point and its lighthouse on its port side, and headed towards a position five miles south-east.

The crew and just three of his close family and one of his old naval mates were on board. The pale, sad face of his widow could be seen as she stood with the ship's Captain, behind the non-reflective glass of the bridge, as the warship slowly cruised to its appointed position. Their marriage had not exactly been steady and close in recent years, but she would not have wished it to end so suddenly and tragically this way.

As the vessel hove-to, slightly rolling in the gentle swell, two midshipmen placed the sealed and weighted wooden casket on a board under the Union Jack, ready for its lowering into the sea. A naval padre conducted a short burial service as the seven people, family and naval, grouped around the guard-rail. A few solitary gulls cried plaintively as they wheeled around the stationary ship. It was a far cry from the thousands of fans that had thronged his shows and concerts just 25 years before.

The service completed, the casket dropped gently into the water and disappeared beneath the waves, followed closely by four wreaths, thrown by the mourners, that bobbed serenely on the surface of the sea, their

H.M.S. Sirius, *which carried David Whitfield's body to burial at sea.*

*The final
moment*

colours in stark contrast to the greyish water. The small group stood silently for a few moments in quiet homage as the wreaths slowly drifted outward towards the four directions of the North Sea. It was a final and personal farewell from the family to the husband and father who, despite setbacks and low periods in his life, had brought happiness to millions of people all over the world with his singing.

Half an hour later a pilot boat took off the civilian party and headed back to the Humber. They were dropped off at Spurn Point and an hour later were back in Hull. The *Sirius*, its job completed, steered south towards its home port of Plymouth, and the casket of ashes settled onto the sea bed below the North Sea. The singing sailor had come back to his home waters.

Thirteen years later, in 1993, in the same month of February, *H.M.S. Sirius* was back again in the port of Hull. This time she had returned on a farewell courtesy visit for a week, prior to sailing for Scotland on her last voyage, to the scrapyard. Strangely, the visit coincided with the official opening of a remembrance rose garden to the same singer whose ashes she had carried to sea so many years before. The Lord Mayor of Hull and other civic dignitaries were there at noon to give the official seal of approval for the garden dedicated to the singer's memory. It would have been his 67th birthday. His widow, members of the family and invited guests, including fans, local artistes and members of the Appreciation Society, who had been responsible for the arrangements, proudly looked on. Not a bad gathering to honour the boy from the back streets of Hull, who had risen to world stardom in the far-away Fifties.

The simple dedication ceremony saw the unveiling of a plaque bearing a verse compiled from some of his most famous song titles. It read: 'I believe, beyond the stars, you'll never walk alone in your dream of paradise, a tear, a kiss and a smile, goodbye.' The city had remembered the singer who was always proud of the place where he was born, lived, and returned to, whenever possible.

He had once remarked that he felt he could always be himself in Hull, go for a pint or a walk, without being bothered. Of course, he would have been the first to admit that his thousands of fans were most important, sometimes, unfortunately, to the detriment of his family, but he would not have a thing said against them. After all, it was the fans who had made him a star. Nevertheless, he said, it was nice, just once in a while, to be able to return to his old easy-going life. This, certainly in his halcyon years, was impossible.

The site of the memorial garden is located on a small strip of land at the corner of Freetown Way and Bourne Street in Hull, just outside the city centre, and on the site of the old Alexandra Theatre which had been bombed during the war. In the garden, behind the plaque, are a hundred specimens of the new rose named after him, which had been introduced

Shiela Whitfield at the dedication of the David Whitfield Rose Garden, 12 February, 1993

IN MEMORY OF
DAVID WHITFIELD

BORN 2 FEBRUARY 1926
DIED 15 JANUARY 1980

I BELIEVE BEYOND THE STARS
YOULL NEVER WALK ALONE
IN YOUR DREAM OF PARADISE
A TEAR A KISS AND A SMILE
GOODBYE

(Picture courtesy Hull Daily Mail)

at the International Flower Show in London two years before.

After the dedication, the group returned to the New Theatre to watch the first showing of vintage film of the singer and other show business personalities, taken in the 1950s on board the new luxury liner, *Empress of Britain*. The video had been specially lent for the occasion by the showman, Hughie Green, who had been largely instrumental in the singer's discovery in 1950.

It was a poignant moment for the people who had known him, and especially for his widow, Shiela, who was with her husband on that occasion many years before. 'I certainly had a lump in my throat,' she said. 'It was strange seeing it for the first time, and it brought back many memories.'

Just over a month later, in March, at the other end of the country, in Portsmouth, a framed photograph of the singer was presented by the Commemorative Society to the King's Theatre in Southsea. This was a theatre that had witnessed many of his solo performances and a summer season over the years. His naval career and many appearances in the city had probably made this his second favourite British city, after his birthplace, Hull. The anecdotes and stories from the City of Portsmouth

H.R.H. Princess Michael of Kent being presented with a David Whitfield rose at the International Flower Show, Hampton Court

are not all flattering, but the vast majority from people of both sexes who remembered his performances and instances of personal kindness seem to bear out his affection for the city.

So, who was this man, still remembered fondly up and down the country and overseas, remembered by men and women, the latter now nearly all grandmothers, who followed him from performance to performance in the comparatively staid days of the mid-Fifties, before the advent of rock and roll? A man who was to break the post-war American monopoly of the record industry; who was the first British male singer to appear in the Top Ten of the U.S.A. hit records, thus winning for himself the first Golden Disc ever awarded to a British singer. A performer who still holds the distinction of being the British artiste with the most appearances on the Ed Sullivan TV show in America.

His name was David Whitfield, and, although it is a very well-worn cliché, his life and career were very much a 'rags to riches' story: a story that at one time in his life almost went into reverse, from 'riches to rags', partly due to his own shortcomings.

The story started in the back streets of Hull at the time of the Depression, reached its peak in the mid-Fifties, fell sharply with the advent of rock and roll and bad publicity, but was on its way up again when he died tragically, at the age of 53, in Australia, on the other side of the world from his native Hull. This is the David Whitfield story.

Chapter Two

Birth and Early Years

David Whitfield was born in Hull to Lillian, generally called Betty, and James Whitfield in February, 1926. He was the third child to be born in the tiny house at No. 3, Albert Terrace, East Street, and was named David after one of his elderly uncles. The Whitfield family, in common with most working families at that time, was a large one. James and Lillian were the eldest two, followed by David, and then five more born in the years between 1924 and 1937. There was another boy in this period but he died almost immediately after birth.

East Street lay in one of the poorer parts of Hull, the area known as Drypool which adjoined the docks. The Whitfield house was surrounded by factories and overlooked a timber yard. This heavy industrial area was surrounded by mills, storehouses and large factories such as those of the British Oil and Cake Mills and Rank's Flour Mills, not the healthiest environment in which to grow up.

It was a generally grey area, on the east bank of the River Hull which flowed into the larger River Humber. A near neighbour of David who lived in the next street describes her house, probably identical to the Whitfield's, as, 'a two up, two down terraced house with a big bay window. There was no front room, just a kitchen and back scullery. The family wouldn't have known the luxury of running hot water or a bathroom. The toilet was outside in a small yard alongside a coalhouse, as nearly all the houses burnt coal for heating and cooking. To take a bath meant using a tin tub

Baby David, 1926

in front of the fire, which was topped up with kettles from the range. The kitchen or cooking area was also very small and it was into this space that the bath was placed. When it was not in use it was either hung up outside in the yard or covered to form a kitchen working surface. In the Whitfield house the "tub" could always be found hanging on a convenient nail on a wall outside.' Not all the 'tubs' were metal, another correspondent mentions 'a wooden tub that had to be put out in the garden, or backyard, soaking in cold water the night before, Friday, so that it didn't leak on the regular bath night, Saturday'.

James Whitfield, David's father, drove a horse and cart around the area collecting and delivering goods, a sort of general purpose carter known as a 'rully' driver in East Yorkshire. Unfortunately, he was often ill, spending a lot of time in hospital, and no work meant no money. He worked for his own father, David's granddad, and, although David was too small to help with the heavy physical work, he could often be seen during school holidays perched on the seat of the cart alongside his father.

Times were very difficult and all the children had to take their share of bringing some money into the family by running errands and doing odd jobs: some of the jobs legal and above board, many of them not quite within the law.

A woman who was about the same age as David writes about the hardship and her early childhood in Hull: 'The Thirties – we were very hard up then. In Stubbing Street there was a second-hand shop called

David, Jimmy and Lillian Whitfield

David, the choirboy, 1936

8

Mary's. We got all we wore, jumpers, shoes, pants etc. from there. Us kids called her "Mucky Mary" – she was not, she washed everything and ironed them before she sold them, but she poured the dirty water down the passage out of the dolly tub when she'd finished, hence our nickname, "Mucky Mary". David would have been four or five when the slump was on. If your sister had some shoes that she'd grown out of, and they kept the weather out, and they fitted you, you wore them. I saw a picture of David once, he must have been about four and he was standing outside the East Street house and he had girls' shoes on.'

David started school when he was five years old and at that time most children, unless they were lucky enough to go to the High School, stayed in the same school until they left to go to work at 14. David's elder sister, Lillian, went on to the High School, probably because she was the eldest, and normally a family of this size could only afford for one child to go. Of course, as in Lily's case, a certain amount of academic ability was also called for. Most of the Whitfield children, including David, went to the same school, except for the youngest three. The school was St. Peter's School, Drypool, in nearby Church Street, and it was here that he was encouraged to begin his singing career by joining the St. Peter's Church Choir.

Although he was inspired by his school teachers, he had already made an acquaintance with the church, as the children were made to go twice every Sunday: not because the Whitfield parents were particularly good church-goers – weddings and funerals were the only time they normally attended – but they were just glad of the opportunity to get rid of the children for a bit of peace on their day of rest.

Mr. Dibner, David's choir-master, soon realised his potential as a singer and gave him extra lessons. In fact, although he was required to attend regular choir practice on Tuesday and Friday evenings, he very often stayed behind for further individual tuition. Only once, when he was eleven years old, did this interest waver. He decided to miss choir practice and go to the cinema with his mates for a change. Perhaps he wanted to be considered one of the boys instead of someone whose life revolved around church choirs. Unfortunately, the choirmaster, thinking that David was ill, sent a boy round to his home to enquire about the health of his young prodigy. His mother was surprised and worried when the boy called. As far as she knew, David had set out as usual for his practice and she had no idea where he had gone. Later that evening when David arrived home he was greeted by both parents who asked him why he was late and where he had been.

'I've been to choir practice,' he replied. He then received the biggest hiding he had ever had: not so much for missing choir practice, but for telling lies. Yorkshiremen tend to be men of their word.

There was no more trouble after this and eventually he became head choir-boy, but he still had no inkling of the professional singing career he was eventually to follow. His main priority when he left school, like the rest of his school mates, would have been to get a job as quickly as possible in one of the many industrial units or in the fishing fleet in order to help bolster the family budget.

As a child, David was fair-haired, strong and wiry. He had to be to survive the hurly burly of the streets and school playground. His sister says: 'Even as a child he knew what he wanted. He was always full of confidence, a real happy-go-lucky lad. Nothing seemed to bother him.'

The usual playground was around the ships and timber yards and, according to his brother, one of his favourite games was to jump through the hatches of the holds of the grain ships into the soft grain below. If he was chased he would disappear into one of the timber yards and climb to the top of one of the wooden stacks where no one could reach him. Another regular game for David and his brothers was to ride on the empty timber bogies. They would direct the small vehicles towards each other and then jump off just before they collided.

Usually, with true boy's luck, he escaped punishment, but once he was well and truly caught. He had been dared to steal one of the dinghies tied alongside the jetty and row it across the harbour. He was halfway across when he noticed three policemen with dogs waiting for him on the other side. He turned back towards where he had come from and saw his mother, looking furious, waiting there. Undecided who would punish him most, he chose to leave it to fate and waited in the middle of the harbour to see what would happen. The question was soon answered. The biggest policeman he had seen in his young life rowed out to collect him, waiting until they were both ashore again before giving him the anticipated clip round the ear.

Even choir boys can get into trouble, although, in the back streets of any big city, a choir boy would not normally be admired by his peers. He was fortunate that he performed well in sports. He always fancied his chances as a fighter and once even considered the possibility of becoming a boxer. Through this talent he was popular at school and at the age when choir singing would have been considered 'girlish' it would have been very handy to be able to flatten any critics. At home he used to enjoy the odd few rounds with his elder brother, Jim. This was probably an opportunity to hit each other without bringing down their mother's wrath, as there was not really any love lost between David and his elder brother throughout boyhood. As in most large families, the children tended to split into rival factions and it seems that David, Doris and Ernie formed one group, with Jim and Lillian in the other.

The nearby docks were not only a place for play. They also served a useful purpose in helping to supplement the family budget. David's younger sister remembers the older members of the family going aboard the ships to recover empty beer bottles from sailors who were either too lazy or too drunk to be bothered to return them themselves. The children hurried off, carrying their clinking bottles, to the nearest pub and collected their refunds. Doris writes: 'We spent a lot of time on the dock until the dock police came with their dogs and then we used to run and jump over this big wall. I shudder when I think of it now, but it was all tough in those days.' Another method of supplementing the family income, usually carried out by the female members of the family, was to beg money from the Swedish sailors off the timber boats as they came ashore to head for the nearest dock-side pub. 'Can you spare a penny, John?' – they were always 'John' to the girls – came the pleading chorus. Apparently this was quite a lucrative sideline and, if they were patient enough to wait until the seamen came out of the pub much later, the donations were much larger in direct proportion to the men's state of drunkenness. The thought does arise of the personal danger of this method of gaining money, but the girls sought safety in numbers, usually forming a group of four or five with their cousins.

David enjoyed his school life, and his popularity with most of the children was shared by the teaching staff. He did reasonably well at school, being interested in most subjects, especially music. One of his old schoolfriends, Ronnie Porte, remembers that most of the children were quite envious of David's singing prowess. It enabled him to dodge some of the lessons for extra practices and almost always put him at the top of the bill in any school stage productions.

His early stage career had its pitfalls because, when he was ten, he was due to sing the *Cobbler's Song* from *Chu-Chin-Chow*. All was ready for the big night, but, on the day before the concert at the dress rehearsal, David decided to swing a large hammer in time to the music to add realism to his song. Unfortunately, he let go at the wrong time and it landed on his foot. By the next day he could not walk. The show went on without him, and he had missed his very first chance of topping the bill.

He had plenty of other chances over his school years. His younger brother, Ted, can remember that when David was 12 he sang an old cowboy song, *Goldmine in the Sky*, at one of the school concerts, so not all his songs had a religious or operatic theme. David's singing was not limited just to school and church. When he was 11 he used to sing in the nearby pubs at Christmas time, bringing in extra money for the festive season food, and making him the truly blue-eyed boy of his mother. Just before Christmas the Whitfield children were issued with a collecting tin, an ordinary can with the top cut off and some thick paper stretched over the top with a slit for the coins. Then they were all sent off around the district to sing carols. According to Doris, all the children wanted to go with David because he always came back with a full tin while the other tins were half empty. But he nearly always insisted on going on his own, and soon made a name for himself around the local pubs. Directly he appeared in the doorway he was lifted up onto the bar where he sang away to his heart's content. Back at home Mum Whitfield sat in the kitchen waiting for the children's return. She would sit with her apron spread out as they returned and tipped the evening's takings into her lap.

Like most boys', David's interest in girls began at school. St. Peter's was a mixed school in the classrooms, although the older children were segregated in the playgrounds, as some of the girls were growing up fast before they left at 14. Some of the older schools still have the 'Girls' and 'Boys' separate entrances marked in concrete above the respective doors. He had a childhood sweetheart in his class who once invited him home to tea, quite a social occasion then, and a sure indication that the 'romance' was fairly serious.

Another of his unusual 'chat-up' methods was to a certain trawler skipper's daughter who was unfortunate enough to sit in front of him in the usual wooden and metal combined desks and benches. With nearly 40 children in each class this did not leave a lot of room. She had five long blonde ringlets hanging down her back and David fell in love with them and the girl. However, he could not resist the temptation to dip each end into the convenient ink-well strategically placed on his own desk. He was sent to the headmaster for a caning for this introduction technique.

Generally, although poor, David and his brothers and sisters had an enjoyable childhood. Times were hard but his mother ensured that no one in the family went hungry and, although the boys of the family were constantly fighting each other, at the end of the day, like most working class families, they were extremely loyal when threatened by outsiders. Like most children in those far-off days, they played nearly all their team games outside in the street. Walls of houses and warehouses were the goalposts and cricket stumps for the endless games of football and cricket, played rigidly according to the appropriate season. Gutters, wet or dry, were useful for marbles, and cigarette cards were avidly saved for the usual playground games. Children's games, as now, tended to follow the seasons. Eastertime was always the skipping season for the girls and for any boy who was daring enough to face the scorn of his mates. Hull being a port, rope was generally easy to come by, and some of these skipping ropes sometimes stretched from one side of the street to the other. The rope was usually thick and heavy so the mothers would occasionally come out and turn it, while a long line of kids jumped up and down.

If the children had a good week collecting money they were allowed to go to the cinema, a real treat. One of the children who knew David well remembers: 'The picture palace was the old Prince's Hall across Queen's Gardens in Dock Street. It was tuppence to get in some cinemas or a penny and a jam-jar at others. Sometimes you got an everlasting goodie lolly and it lasted two days. It was just like a big boiled sweet, mostly blackcurrant. We all paid a penny to see Tom Mix, Roy Rogers and Ben Turpin. There were penny rushforms inside, not seats like now. We'd all jump up and down at the "goodies" and "baddies". I remember a woman made toffee apples, a halfpenny each, and they were sticky and it was all over our faces, and a man was taking photos from Jerome's in Whitefriargate and David had toffee all over his face and he wiped it across his sleeve; he looked like Al Jolson with his blond hair and the sticky toffee.'

David had several boyhood friends that he still kept in touch with during his years of stardom. One in particular still lives in Hull, and, although he was slightly older than David, they became boyhood friends partly because of the friendship of their mothers, and partly because they lived very close to each other. One of David's earliest memories was of calling at the house of this friend to pick him up to go to the local baths for a Saturday morning swim. He knocked at the door which was opened by the boy's mother.

'Can Ronnie come out to go to the swimming baths?' asked David politely.

'He's not going to any swimming baths until he can swim,' was her retort as she slammed the door.

David always remembered her answer and still chuckled to himself years after, especially as they both finished up in the Navy. This same friend also remembers the time they looked forward for weeks to a film showing at the local cinema entitled, *The Prince of Wales*. They queued up for an hour to see the film, thinking it was going to be an animal adventure film, but were bitterly disappointed to find it was all about the Royal Family. Obviously some of their English education had been missed along the way!

By 1936 the Whitfield family had grown considerably. The three eldest, James, Lily and David, had been joined by Doris, Ernie, Ted and Keith, and the youngest, Geoff, was on the way.

A move to a larger house was on the cards and they moved to Harcourt Street. This was not just a larger house but it had a large wide yard as well, ideal for the football matches that the brothers organised. David's father was still very poorly and a lot of the sparse income coming into the house was provided by the older children using their native wit to provide pennies for food.

In 1938, the family moved again, to Beaumont Street, the first time that they possessed the status symbol of a front garden. This move coincided with Jimmy, the eldest, going out to work, so his extra wage packet must have made a big difference. Unbeknown to the family, the threat of war was beginning to loom and by the end of that war all their lives, and David's in particular, were going to be altered for ever.

Chapter Three

The Early War Years

When David was 13, in 1939, the country went to war. It was to be a bloody, bitter war for the people of Hull, as the port, like many others on the south and east coasts of England, became the target for what seemed like an unceasing wave after wave of German bombers. The docks and industrial units were obvious targets for the enemy planes, along with the adjoining airfields, and the people of Hull, living in close proximity to these, were badly affected.

It was David's final year at school and attendance was cut to half days for the younger children. In the winter months the majority of children went and returned from their schools in the dark, as there were no street lights to show the way. A great deal of school time was spent with the children running to and fro the air-raid shelters. Lessons consisted mainly of listening to and telling stories in the damp semi-darkness of those rough concrete structures.

Schooling was a hazardous business in the first years of the war, running the risks of bombs, anti-personnel mines, incendiary devices and shrapnel, the latter eagerly collected by David and his mates. They had learnt to detect the whereabouts of the biggest pieces by looking for impact marks on areas with short cut grass. The most collectable prize was the tail fins of an incendiary bomb. It was worth at least four pieces of shrapnel.

The adult population were also catered for by the provision of shelters from the bombs. They were provided to stop the impact from blast, flying shrapnel and falling buildings, the consequence and aftermath of the air-raids, as a direct, or near direct, hit would have been as fatal to anyone as staying in the house. Those with gardens, even of postage stamp size, were issued with Anderson shelters that were half buried in what was once the vegetable plot. Householders without the necessary space had to use the large communal shelters built in the streets.

Most of the raids occurred at night. It was not so common to experience a daytime raid but there were plenty of false alarms. People emerged from their shelters in the early morning gloom to check that electricity supplies were still available after the night's raids. If not, out would come the candles and paraffin lamps. If cooking facilities were available, breakfast was usually porridge; otherwise it was bread and beef dripping, as all other items were rationed and had to be eked out to last the entire week. Air raid warning sirens sounded at the first signs of enemy aircraft approaching but people, like those in most big cities, got an uncanny knack of detecting early the sound of the aircraft and the possibility of an air-raid. As Mrs. H. remembers: 'Sometimes we were well aware of an impending air attack long before the sirens sounded – it was like a sixth sense.'

The Whitfield family, now numbering ten, Mam and Dad and their eight children, were now living at Beaumont Street, following the move the year before the war started. Children of school age, including David, Ted, Ernie and Doris, were evacuated to Scarborough, a seaside town that was considered slightly safer than the industrial towns. The exceptions were Lily and Jim, the eldest, who was shortly to go into the Merchant Navy. They stayed with their father in Hull along with their two youngest brothers, Keith and Geoff, who were considered too young to leave their mother.

David's good looks and opportunism soon made him popular with his temporary landlady. He remembered supplementing the house meat ration by bringing home an unfortunate duck that he had spotted walking across the road from a nearby pond. However, a lull in the bombing, and the fact that David soon became old enough to leave school meant quite a swift return for the four children. They were re-united with their mother and the two youngest at Morley, near Leeds and later they stayed in a small town, Ardsley, also in Yorkshire.

David's first full-time job, after leaving school, was as an errand and delivery boy for a Jewish baker, and he spent most of his working day pedalling his way around the narrow streets. He was not paid very much, but his wages were very welcome in the Whitfield household at a very difficult time. David was allowed to keep a shilling for pocket money and to make a little extra on Saturday, the Jewish Sabbath, his day off, when he spent his time cleaning and polishing his boss's bread van.

Sunday mornings were particularly busy for the young David, when he began his bread deliveries at six o'clock in the morning. He normally delivered a large quantity of small Jewish loaves, known as 'bogles' (bagels), in a huge basket carried at the front of his carrier bicycle. The memory of the hot sweet- smelling rolls must have lingered because he always had a liking for these right through to his show business days. A girl who grew up in the next street to the Whitfield's remembers: 'Even in the darkest days of the war, the foodshops always had an aroma of well-being, with the smell of freshly baked bread, crusty rolls and soft baps.

These we bought on our way to school for a halfpenny. If we wanted margarine as well, it cost us a penny. To eat these "cakes" on the way to school was luxury, as sweets and fruit were definitely things of the past for most of the younger children. Many of us didn't even know what they looked like, let alone their taste.'

Like the errand boy, Granville, in the television series, *Open all Hours*, David was always in a hurry. Much more interesting things were waiting for his off-duty hours. In his haste to complete his deliveries in the shortest possible time he sometimes fell off his bike, spilling the loaves all over the wet road. He then had to go back to the shop to face the irate Mr. Freedman and to pick up another load. Part of his haste on a Sunday was probably because he knew that, after the early morning job was completed, he had to hurry to church to sing in the choir.

David and his father used to stand in their front garden, watching the bombers come swooping in over the coast, using the River Humber as a pointer to the industries and airfields close inland. Very often they were forced to run for shelter if the bombs came too close. The family were bombed out twice in the early Forties. Both times they were lucky enough to be in the safety of a shelter. After the second occasion, which only resulted in the windows being blown in and some superficial damage, they were forced to stay in a local chapel before being returned to their home. The first bombing was the worst as the house was completely gutted and they were forced to move again, this time to Lorraine Street to a house which is still standing. David's younger sister, Doris, remembered being quite upset about this move because, up to then, 'My sister and I always had our own bedroom, away from the boys. It was only when we moved to Lorraine Street that it was hard. There were ten of us and so we had to share. I suppose that's all we could get as everyone was being bombed out.'

David's bakery delivery job was followed by several others as he became older, bigger and stronger. He helped his father with the horse and cart delivery service but it soon became obvious there was hardly enough work for one, let alone two. His wiriness and strength became very useful when he got a job pushing a handcart for Flowers Transport, delivering general goods around the neighbourhood. There were plenty of job vacancies in the factories at the time but David much preferred the outdoor life. In any case, he could sing away to his heart's content outside without offending too many people. It is doubtful whether he could have done the same in a factory.

David knew many songs by heart, some from school and his choir days, but many from the famous tenor, Richard Tauber, who was a great inspiration to him. Friends said that, when David included several Italian language songs in his repertoire, he probably did not know what the words meant, but he deserved praise for learning them by heart. Tauber actually visited Hull just before the war and one of David's friends arranged for him to meet him, but he was too scared, or shy, to go. He always regretted never meeting the great man.

In 1942, David began his semi-professional singing career, apart from his pre-Christmas carol singing exploits. A lady whose husband was the Secretary at the Perth Street Club in Hull during the Second World War takes up the story: 'One night when the club ran out of beer, it was rationed then, a party of us went to see a friend of ours, called Len Palen: he was compère at the Boating Club in Stoneferry, just behind The Grapes public house. When we got there, they too had run out of beer, but we got some from the pub.

During the evening Len got a young boy up to sing. It was David. He was very shy and took a lot of persuading, but he sang really great, we all thought he would become a very good artiste. Before we left my husband offered him a booking at the Perth Street Club. He refused at first as he was really shy, but an uncle offered to come with him, so it was arranged. This was, as far as I know, his first booking and he was paid seven and sixpence (37p) in the old money.

On the said evening he sang so well, Arthur rang Fred Porter at the Dixon's Arms, Woodmansey, and he gave him his second booking, and that's how David started. I can remember two of the songs he sang, *Hear My Song, Violetta,* and *Goodbye* from the musical *White Horse Inn.*'

As David's singing bookings were still few and far between, at this time, he was forced to renew his acquaintance with a horse and cart in his next job, when he worked as a coalman's mate for Rafferty and Watson of Hull. Yet another outdoor job that enabled him to sing his way around Hull and the surrounding area.

In the early 1940's two very important things happened that were to influence David's life for the next seven years. His father died in the Driffield Base Hospital, just outside Hull, in 1942, when David was 16. He had undergone a succession of operations for stomach ulcers, 14 in all, and suffered many years of pain and discomfort. The three eldest children, including David, were left as the family breadwinners. Life became really hard immediately after the father's death and Mrs. Whitfield was forced to go to the 'parish' for assistance. The situation got slightly better once Doris left school. It was decided that she and Lily would help by alternately staying at home to look after the younger children to enable their mother to go out to work as she, being older and more experienced in the job, could earn more money than her daughters. There was even enough for them to be able to receive a small payment every week for their housekeeping duties.

Also, in 1943, David decided to join the Royal Navy. He was now 17 and, as he would soon have been drafted into the Army or the Air Force, the Navy seemed the better option, especially as he had been working on a tug, the *Marksman,* for the past couple of months. It turned out to be the right decision for many reasons that will become apparent as his story unfolds.

Acceptance into the R.N. was not automatic even in those war days and David went off to the local recruitment office at Chapel Street full of hope. Strangely enough, he was the only member of the family to join the Royal Navy. His elder brother was already in the Merchant fleet and his older sister in the A.T.S. Doris , the younger sister, was in the Land Army at the end of the war, while most of the brothers did National Service in the Army, except for Keith who signed on as a Regular.

As the recruiting office was at the other side of the city, he borrowed his younger brother Ted's bicycle, a paper round bike belonging to a local shop. He was so pleased when he was accepted that he forgot the bike and left it behind at the recruiting office. When he went back it had disappeared. His younger brother and the newsagent were not amused.

A few weeks later, David left 6, Florence Grove, Lorraine Street, and

headed south to begin his basic training. He did not know at that moment, but, by the time he was demobbed in seven years time, his life would be drastically altered and he would be on the path to stardom that inevitably would steer his future in a direction that he would not have believed possible.

One of his reasons for joining the Navy was to be able to travel. He certainly did that, but the journey was also going to provide the initial thrust to his travelling much wider, as an international singing star. That, however, was in the future. There was a little account to settle with Adolf Hitler first.

Teenage David, 1943

Chapter Four

Life in the Royal Navy

His basic training was carried out at Portsmouth, on the South Coast. This would have been quite a step for him, as before this he had never been further from home than Scarborough, as an evacuee. He took to the service life straight away and was to remain in the Navy for seven years, although he could have been demobbed after four. At that time, the prospects of a signing-on fee of £32 and another £100 when he finally left persuaded him to sign on for another three years. In any case, by the time his service had nearly been completed, he was having the time of his life in the Far East.

Looking back over David's life, including his years of top stardom, it is probably true to say that his happiest years were spent in the Royal Navy. He got fed, paid and generally looked after, travelled to parts of the world that he had only dreamt about and, above all, managed to continue with his singing. This contentment is borne out by the way in later years, when he was a star, he was never too busy to welcome his old shipmates to his dressing room, always insisting on a later meeting after the show, to talk over old times. One such ex-seaman served with David in the mid-Forties and says: 'Some years later I went to see him on the local Hippodrome and at the end of his act he called for any old shipmates to see him after the show. Knowing him I was sure it was a genuine request but I couldn't bring myself to do so, much to the disappointment of my wife.' David also welcomed the special camaraderie to be found in all the services, probably mostly so in the Navy, and later expected the same sort of comradeship in show business, but, unfortunately, on a lot of occasions he was bitterly disappointed.

It was during his time in the Navy that the name of his future wife, Shiela Priestman, crops up. He had obviously seen her before as she lived at the other end of Lorraine Street in Hull, but at that time she would have been just a skinny young school-girl, more likely to have been friendly with one of his younger brothers. During one of his leaves in 1945 he happened to see a young, pretty, dark-haired girl waiting at a bus stop, and

he was determined to ask her out. It was Shiela. It was not quite as simple as it seemed, because it turned out that she was only 13 at the time, and her parents did not exactly welcome the prospect of their young only child going out with a 19-year-old- sailor. He finally plucked up courage to ask her to go out to the pictures and she agreed, but there was still her father to convince. After a lot of persuasion he consented but insisted that she should be home by ten o'clock. David readily agreed; anything to get her to go out with him. Their first date was at the Regal Cinema in Hull. Unfortunately, the programme was a long one and it was almost ten o'clock when they came out of the cinema. The expensive, but absolutely necessary, answer was a taxi that got her home with seconds to spare and gave David the opportunity to take her out again.

His younger brother, Ted, remembers some of the times David returned home on leave after he had been abroad. On one occasion he brought home a tin of bananas. Most of the family's children had never seen them before and did not know what they were, let alone how to eat them. Not to be outdone, brother Jim returned home with a Luger pistol, as a war souvenir. This rapidly disappeared from one of the household drawers and was never seen again. Jim also brought home a pet monkey. There was obviously never a dull moment in the Whitfield household when the brothers came home on leave. Ted can remember the monkey tearing the back off a soft armchair and making a bed in it. It used to stay in there for most of the time. We are not told the reaction of David's mother.

David served on several ships, including *Ramillies, Concorde, Belfast* and the *Black Swan.* He finished his time at *H.M.S. Vernon*, the torpedo ratings training base at Portsmouth. At this barracks a brass plaque was later put above one of the dormitory beds bearing the legend: 'David Whitfield slept here 1950'. A few years later, after he had left the service,

David was appearing in a variety show at Southsea when he met a matelot at a service football match.

'Aren't you David Whitfield?' he enquired. 'Don't you know they've got a plaque over your old bunk at *Vernon*?' 'I couldn't believe it,' said David. 'So off we went to see it. When I got there, there were only four holes in the woodwork.' The occupant of the bed had got a draft and taken the plaque with him. Fortunately, it was recovered in later years after David's death and now graces part of the display at the small David Whitfield museum in Hull.

His first ship was the ancient battleship *Ramillies* and, as a seaman gunner, he saw action on D-Day, carrying out a bombardment of the beaches prior to the landing of the Allied forces. Even with the possibility of German air attack this would have been a vastly preferable task to that of the army in storming the beaches on foot. At the end of the war, the old *Ramillies* was sent for scrap and David tried to buy the ship's bell as a memento. He was unlucky. It is very likely that a high ranking officer beat him to it!

Aboard the various ships and establishments David carried on singing, not only to entertain the officers and crews but, whenever he got the opportunity, to sing in clubs and bars ashore, both at home and abroad. He travelled to the Far East, to North Africa and to the U.S.A., the country he was to visit often later when he became a star.

The reaction to his continual singing from his shipmates was not always appreciative. One of his former mates on the *Black Swan* wrote: 'My first meeting with David was rather funny. I'd gone to the shower-room for my nightly dhobeying (washing clothes) and shower and there was this chap giving out quite a good rendition of *Goodbye* from the *White Horse Inn*. The others in the bath-house weren't so impressed as they were unable to talk because of his loud booming voice. They were all yelling at him to "pipe down" or "stow it", or they'd fit a bucket over his head. However, it didn't seem to deter him and he carried on singing at the top of his voice. As time went on I must admit I got a bit tired of *Goodbye*, which was his favourite song in a very limited repertoire.'

Another of his mess-mates who served with him in the shore base H.M.S. *Vernon* remembers the same powerful voice booming out from the bathhouse with the same reaction from the other men taking a shower. This time David had an answer for them. 'One day this voice will make me famous, and you'll have to pay to hear it,' he replied. It sounded rather arrogant then ,but it shows just how determined he was to break into professional show business.

David was appreciated much more ashore. His shipmates thought he had finally gone round the bend when he spent over a month's pay on a white sharkskin dinner jacket to enhance his appearance at his performances ashore in Hong Kong. It turned out to be a very good investment because it was here that his personal club appearances and short radio show gave him the confidence to move on to bigger things in later years.

At the beginning of 1947 David was serving on a captured German destroyer that had been re-named *H.M.S. Nonsuch* and was anchored in the harbour at Portsmouth. One of his old shipmates remembers that David was not always super-confident and in the early days much preferred singing to himself: 'Our job was simply maintenance, and David, always singing, echoed beautifully in a half empty ship. His favourites then were *Marta, The Drinking Song* and *Come Back to Sorrento*. I was one of many who urged him to do something about that voice and he told me he'd been on Carol Levis's Discoveries and failed miserably. Incidentally, I only ever knew him as "Yorkie" Whitfield.

'He was in great demand at camp concerts and the powers-to-be refused his repeated requests for a foreign draft. I later joined another ship which was nearby and I got "Yorkie" to come aboard, hoping he'd sing for my new shipmates but for once he was too shy.'

In April 1947 he was sent to the Royal Naval Barracks at Portsmouth to wait for a foreign service draft. His request had finally been granted. Not many sailors enjoyed their stay in the Barracks; there was too much bull and spit and polish, and the normal routine was to volunteer for anything just to get out and David was no exception. His draft came through in a reasonably short time, a transfer to the cruiser *Belfast* in Singapore.

He left Liverpool on the *Empress of Scotland* in late May bound for the Far East. It was a passenger liner carrying a large number of Army and R.A.F. personnel but only 25 naval ratings. Much to David's delight, a concert party was formed to entertain the civilian and service passengers during the long voyage. Apart from his usual solo performances he sang a duet with a young lady passenger who was going out to join her husband in Hong Kong. The singing sailor was beginning to appear before a

On the Empress of Scotland *sailing to Singapore to join H.M.S. Belfast, May 1947*

22

much wider audience, even if he was still singing for fun. His early choir boy training and appearances before live audiences in Hull and Portsmouth were beginning to stand him in good stead.

The liner reached Singapore in the middle of June, when one of his fellow sailors, and a good friend of David, reached the age of 19, still a year too young to receive his tot of rum. He remembers the ever friendly David giving him half of his tot in way of celebration. A truly magnificent gesture, as rum was more valuable than gold in the Royal Navy. The *Belfast* was at sea when the liner docked so David and the rest of the naval contingent were sent to *H.M.S. Simbang*, the Naval Air Station on Singapore Island, to await the arrival of their ship. Three weeks later, during which time David and one of his mates painted most of the base fire station, the *Belfast* arrived in harbour. They hastily transferred to the ship and sailed for Hong Kong in a matter of days. From Hong Kong the vessel was due to go home so David was drafted to a much smaller ship, the frigate, *Black Swan.*

He had the reputation of being a bit of a loner on this ship as most of his off-duty hours in 1947 and 1948 were spent singing in clubs and bars.

On the few occasions that he did go ashore for a drink he tended to go with one or other rating instead of a large crowd. One of his run ashore 'oppos' remembers when David was invited to dinner by an English couple in Shanghai, one of the perks of his cabaret appearances, and he was invited to go with him: 'We worked our way through the noise and clamour of early evening in Shanghai to the address he'd been given. Eventually, we arrived at the door of a house that looked old worldly and had seen better days, in a rather inconspicuous side street. Once we were admitted the change was astounding. As the door was shut behind us it was as if someone had found an "off" switch to the noise outside. We were ushered through

At Wanchia, Hong Kong, c.1947-8

23

french doors onto a patio overlooking a small garden. It was as peaceful and tranquil as if we were standing in an English country garden. Of course, being sailors, when asked what we wanted to drink, we chose beer. The Shanghai Breweries turned out some pretty potent stuff, but it never tasted as good as it did then. It was served ice-cold in wafer-thin silver tankards and to us, sweating in our white suits, hot and clammy after our hectic journey, it tasted like pure nectar. The meal was in best English tradition too: roast lamb, roast potatoes, cauliflower, peas and mint sauce. All in all a very memorable evening.' It certainly paid to be friendly with the singing sailor and this particular friend met David many years later at Bournemouth and had an equally 'memorable evening', which will be mentioned in a later chapter.

A little known fact that only came to light with the recent publication of Kenneth Williams' diaries was that he and David were friendly while they were both serving in Hong Kong in 1947. Kenneth Williams was in the Army and due for demob and obviously met David at some form of services concert because he writes about his fabulous singing voice. They corresponded by letter for the next year after Kenneth returned home and then the friendship seems to have ceased. Although the comedy actor was a self-confessed homosexual, it is hardly likely that David was the same, given his track record with the female sex, before and after this episode, and for the rest of his life.

Kenneth Williams seemed to be a very lonely person and David was always over-friendly, and to a matelot abroad, not particularly well paid, the opportunity to have someone buy the drinks all evening, with no strings attached, was probably very welcome. A rather sad footnote to the friendship was that the letters from David ceased some time in 1948 and apparently some years later David publicly snubbed the actor in a London restaurant.

One of David's most regular bookings ashore during 1947 and 1948 was with a small nine-piece dance band formed in Hong Kong by Ken Cochrane. David started with the band as the interval cabaret turn. He sang while the rest of the band, with the exception of the pianist, had half an hour's break. He was forced to increase his collection of songs, and his rich, tenor voice began to perform staple tenor favourites like *Come Back to Sorrento* and *I'll Take You Home Again, Kathleen.*

The band and David became very popular in the Colony, performing at most of the clubs, including the Kowloon Cricket Club and the China Fleet Club. They were also in great demand for dinners and functions by the St. John's Church Cheerio Club, The Stanley Prison Warders Club and the Dockyard Social Club.

When the band-leader was looking for a cabaret show to partner the band at functions he managed to persuade a group of singers called Tex Winter and the Tumbleweeds to work with them. This group was formed from serving naval personnel and David was one of them. He would never have believed, five years previously, that his singing career would eventually take off in China, on the other side of the world from his native Hull.

Ken Cochrane found David a very likeable person although a bit shy and reserved. He did, however, as usual, have an eye for the ladies. While he was performing with the band he became rather interested in the young daughter of one of the group. The father came to Ken and asked him to warn David off, 'as he didn't want his daughter to associate with a common matelot'. The band leader told the Dad to get lost and tell him himself and the 'romance' gradually faded of its own accord. A few years after this David became a world star and was making quite a lot of money. That father must have kicked himself ever since.

With the Ken Cochrane Band, 1948

At the China Fleet Club, 1947

25

Chapter Five

The Singing Sailor

While David was on the *Black Swan* in 1948 he found his singing career beginning to develop even more. Although he was paid by the Navy it seemed that more and more of his time was spent ashore entertaining. Apart from his regular stints with Ken's band he managed to wangle a week's leave and spent the time singing at the Cock and Pullet nightclub in Hong Kong, where the white tuxedo came in handy, and he also had a regular programme on Radio Hong Kong(ZBW). The slot consisted of a 15-minute singing session for which he was paid £8, nearly a fortnight's pay as an Able Seaman.

With all this extra money coming in, David should have been pretty well off, but, like all matelots, paid once a fortnight, he eagerly awaited pay day. Not that he always needed money: his voice was very often his fortune. One of his mess-mates aboard the *Black Swan* recalls: ' On one of our many trips up the China coast we were invited to a social evening by the Ladies of Amoy and, owing to duties, David and I were late getting ashore and we both discovered that we were not very flush (cash-wise). "Not to worry," says David. "We won't go short of a drink or two," and, believe me, we didn't, once he gained the attention of all the females present with his singing.'

Another crew member, now living in the U.S.A. recollects 'David singing in the canteen at *H.M.S. Terror,* the shore base at Singapore. There were six or seven of us and we all got a pint each for his efforts. This was between Boxing Day and New Year's Eve in 1948 and was most welcome as we didn't get paid until New Year's Eve.' So,it was very useful to have David Whitfield on your ship, if only to keep you supplied with free beer.

He still had to perform his normal naval duties which, because of his gunnery training, usually consisted of guarding various service dignitaries. On one occasion the *Black Swan* had the task of taking the new Governor to Sarawak and during the welcoming firework display David's legs were badly burnt. This put paid temporarily to his singing

H.M.S. Black Swan, *Hong Kong, 1947*

ashore, as he had to spend three weeks in the sick bay. When the trouble broke out in Malaya with the Chinese communists, the *Black Swan* was one of the first ships to be sent to back up the 'virgin soldiers'. David was detailed as one of the armed escort to take the Captain and First Lieutenant of the ship cross-country by road to meet the C-in-C. This was probably one of the few times that he did not feel like singing, as the countryside was swarming with enemy forces and he would not have been popular for attracting attention to the escort's whereabouts.

He left the *Black Swan* at the end of 1948, having volunteered to be a medical guinea- pig at the naval base *H.M.S. Terror* in Singapore. He was attached to the Tropical Research Unit at the base, working with doctors carrying out research on living conditions in the tropics. It was possible to earn extra money to do this, but it surely must have been in David's mind as well that the possibility of being based ashore, and of extra leave, would be much more convenient for his prospective singing career. During his tour of duty in the Far East, David gave way to naval tradition by becoming tattooed. He had three tattoos on each arm. He said on more than one occasion later that he hated them, but he never made any attempt to hide them or get them removed.

While he was singing for servicemen at the Y.M.C.A. in Hong Kong an American entertainer and M.C. at one of the clubs, Glada Strode, heard him sing. She was so impressed that she wrote to the Commander in Chief suggesting that Able Seaman David Whitfield be discharged from the Royal Navy, as she felt, 'he would give much more pleasure to servicemen and civilians by singing full-time'. The Admiral's comments have not been recorded but we can imagine his reaction. However, his Divisional Officer did tell him about the letter and told him that the Navy still wished to retain his services but added, 'Be patient, some day that voice of yours will make you famous.'

Most of his service in the Far East was spent in Singapore and even here he still managed to find time to entertain both servicemen and civilians. A lot of early stage experience was gained which was to prove invaluable in his later career. He once said in a radio interview in Humberside, long after his world-wide success with *Cara Mia*, that there

was really no such thing as an overnight success in show business. It had to be worked at for years; bearing in mind that David had been singing since he was a small boy both as an amateur, semi-professional and professional, he was undoubtedly right.

Another aspect of David's character is evident from his time in Singapore: his great affection for children. A man who was ten years old in 1949 remembers that the children of civilians and servicemen were allowed to use the swimming pool in the naval base *H.M.S. Terror*. He recalls a certain sentry at the establishment who always had time to talk to the children and sometimes even sing to them: his name was David Whitfield.

David returned to England at the end of 1949, expecting great things after his relative success abroad, and he was stationed for a while near Southampton. Talent shows were all the rage at the time and

On sentry duty, Singapore

there was enough hopeful talent in the area for the shows to appear weekly at the local theatre. David applied for an audition, was accepted, and sang on the stage the same night. The song he chose was *Come Back to Sorrento* and, as he neared the end of the song, the applause was so great that he was unable to finish it. Unfortunately, the audience's enthusiasm had the opposite effect to what they, and he, wanted, and he was disqualified. The contest stipulated that every act had to be completed and a very disappointed rating returned to his base.

David always had the knack of bouncing back and he was never down-hearted for long. His tough upbringing in the back streets of Hull had prepared him for most of the kicks in life. His solution was to go out and sing, even if it was only in the pubs of Portsmouth, where he is still remembered. 'David Whitfield was a name I knew, a voice I knew, but, alas, not a man I knew. I well remember visiting the White Hart public house on the corner of Kingston Crescent and Kingston Road, now a branch of the Bradford and Bingley. It was in the late 40's. I visited this pub from time to time, always enjoying the happy atmosphere. Music was played on the piano accordion by a real character by the name of Bert. I learnt in later years that Bert was a serving matelot. On one visit we were all chatting, partly oblivious to Bert's music, when suddenly there came this fantastic voice singing over the general hubbub of the bar. All the noise ceased for this uniformed sailor, the later famous David Whitfield. His singing was enjoyed on many visits after that, always to a packed bar. Mr. Glover, the landlord, must have been well pleased; so were we!' writes a Whitfield fan from the early days who still lives in the city.

It seemed that fate was beginning to conspire against him in his ambition to become a professional singer, and David was beginning to resign himself to returning to Hull, marrying Shiela and settling down to a normal day-time job, when in early 1950, while he was waiting for demobilisation, the event occurred that was ultimately to change his life.

David was stationed at *H.M.S. Vernon,* the training base for torpedo ratings but he, as a gunner, was part of the barrack guard. According to David, he used to go into the W.R.N.S. quarters for a cup of tea, 'as the tea in there was much better than the N.A.A.F.I. tea'. A likely story! As one of the Wren stewards based at *Vernon* at the time remembers: 'Anyway, there was this blond, blue-eyed sailor, cheekily asking me for a cuppa. It was all against the rules and regulations for any sailor to be near or at the Nissen hut, and there he was, full of himself, and me meekly letting him come in to have a cup of tea. It was during the tea-break any way, and a few girls were in having their tea, and, of course, that's what it was, a chance to chat the girls up.' He got very friendly with two of the W.R.N.S. who had heard him sing many times. One of the girls now lives in Australia and was based in *Vernon* as a general steward in 1950. She remembers David very well. She describes David as 'loving women, his drink, and playing darts up at the pubs, a real man's man. Tall, blond and ruggedly handsome – we were all overcome by him.' He did actually become very fond of one of the W.R.N.S., a rather sophisticated Chelsea girl, and was in two minds about this romance and his girl back in Hull, whom he had known all his life.

Wherever David was, entertainment was never far away and, as the steward could play the piano, she suggested that they get together to put on a small show for the lads at the barracks, and, of course, he was quite happy to do this. In the meantime she had noticed, on a shopping expedition in Portsmouth, a rather outdated tatty poster advertising an 'Opportunity Knocks' programme to be held at the Theatre Royal. The heats were to be held in a small dance-hall on the other side of the city and were due to take place during the second half of the evening, after the dance. It took a great deal of persuasion to win over David to go to the audition as he was not a keen dancer, but she convinced him that all he had to do was sit around and have a few pints until the competition began. He went off with his two female escorts and his music, the song *Goodbye,* and waited fairly patiently for the talent show to start. There was still a final hitch to David's 'discovery'. One of the W.R.N.S. went off to find the manager of the hall, leaving a disgusted, impatient David and his companion with their soft drinks: the hall was unlicensed. When she eventually found the compère, his shattering reply was: 'Sorry but we're full right up with talent, and any way you should have put his name down weeks ago.'

'You don't know what you're missing. This fellow has a fantastic voice,' pleaded his backer. 'You will never forgive yourself if you don't give him a chance.'

After a lot of pleading and cajoling – the ex-Wren admits that she was very good at that – the manager told her to get David to sit by the stage door area and, if one of the competitors did not turn up, he could take their place. Joan, his friend, takes up the story from there: 'David was very fed up by this time, and just wanted to get out and go for a drink, so it took all my willpower to hold him to his seat. The show started with people being introduced and coming out front to do their act and it seemed to go on for ever. The door next to the stage suddenly opened and a man beckoned to David to come in. The next thing David was on stage giving his music to the pianist and he started to sing. Well, he won, didn't he? The crowd went wild and the manager stepped up on stage and said, "To think I nearly turned this young man away." '

Events just seemed to take charge after that. David sang at the rehearsals for the show at the Theatre Royal on the following Monday and then appeared in the all-winners night on the Saturday. Half of the Navy seemed to be there that night to cheer him on and, whether it helped or not, he won the grand final. Hughie Green, who was then running the show *Opportunity Knocks* on Radio Luxembourg, met David and asked him to contact him when he was demobbed as he wanted to take him on his touring show around Britain. It seemed that the 'singing sailor' was finally on his way into full-time show business.

The good news swiftly travelled back to his home town, as an article in the *Hull Times* dated 20 May 1950 shows: 'Listeners to the *Opportunity Knocks* programme on Radio Luxembourg tomorrow will hear a Hull man, David Whitfield, aged 24, of Sutton View, Lorraine St., taking part in the allwinners contest. He has almost completed 7 years in the Royal Navy and is due to be demobilised next month. Mr. Whitfield, who is a tenor, sang *Goodbye* from *White Horse Inn* at the recording of the programme in London earlier in the week and was judged winner by the studio audience's applause. The final result rests with the voting of the listeners.'

With Hughie Green on Radio Luxembourg

Chapter Six

The Beginning (1950 – 1953)

The meeting with Hughie Green turned out to be the catalyst that sparked off the Whitfield singing career and his eventual meteoric rise to stardom. When he was released from the Navy, the *Hull Daily Mail* had as a headline, 'Demob! David Whitfield returned to Civvy Street in June 1950 after a long spell at Singapore where he broadcast before he came back to the U.K. in August 1949.' Just after his release, he toured with the *Opportunity Knocks* show for eight months and also broadcast on Radio Luxembourg, a station which was listened to, avidly, by millions at the beginning of the Fifties. It is a strange thought that both Tony Hancock and Alma Cogan were turned down by the same show at about this time.

While he was on tour he spent a period at the Metropolitan Theatre, Edgeware Road, and it was there he met one of the many girls who were to fall under his spell throughout his stage career, Doreen Sturgeon. Although she was only 16, like David she was star-struck and keen for a career on the 'boards'. They appeared in the same show, he was a tenor, she was the female part of a mind-reading act. They soon became very friendly, and eventually David stayed in 'digs' at her parents' house in London. She was one of twins, and her sister, apparently, went out with the comedian, Terry Scott; they often used to form a foursome to go for a drink after the show. One thing led to another and Doreen, now pregnant, ran away from home to join David in Wales. He was appearing in Garnet, near Merthyr Tydfil, at the time. However, Doreen's mother could not really visualise David as a prospective son-inlaw and she went to South Wales with Doreen's brother to fetch her back. Doreen and David's daughter, Madeleine, was born in London in April 1951. Later in the year Doreen read in a newspaper that David and Shiela had married in Hull. He had gone back to his home-town sweetheart, some say to improve his womanising image and to settle, although that was not the only reason; there is little doubt that he loved his new wife. He and Shiela did, however, pay maintenance to his daughter for many years, until Doreen married and Madeleine was adopted by her step-father.

David's contract with Hughie Green continued and he must have thought that this time he was really on his way in show business. But it was not to be quite yet. The tour ended and, for the first time for many years, he was out of a job. He went back to his native Hull and worked as a coalman's mate for a while. Shiela had her own hair-dressing business in Gipsyville on the outskirts of the city, and often, during a pause in his rounds, David would walk into the salon for a cup of tea. The astonished customers peered out from below their domed hair-driers, wondering who the young man covered in coal-dust could be.

During this period David did not give up singing altogether. He must have been very disappointed, but it did not show. He was as ever the super optimist and his confidence that one day he would make the professional grade stayed with him.

One of his best friends was a butcher by day, Ted Turner, who had great faith in David's prowess as a singer. To encourage him he used his car as a taxi to transport David around the city and to the neighbouring seaside resorts to perform at the various clubs, pubs and summer talent shows. He was never short of part-time bookings but the big prize still

Back at Work, 1953   *(Photograph by the late Donald I. Innes.*
Innes Studio, Hessle)

33

eluded him. Despite his taxi-driving friend's efforts it seemed that his professional singing career had come to an end. David's next daytime job was in a pre-cast stone maker's yard. The work was long and arduous but it was worth more money. Sometimes he worked from six in the morning to nine at night, so his part-time singing dates suffered.

His job at the yard was to make breeze blocks, the first time they had been manufactured in Hull. A mixture of cement and cinders was fed into a small machine that had only recently been introduced to the firm. The breeze blocks were experimental and were being used for the erection of internal walls for the vast re-building programme going on in the country at that time. The experiment was obviously a success as the same type of blocks are still being used today.

Several of his old work-mates still remember him before and after the time he became a star, including his foreman: 'He was always singing and was a good-natured man, a pleasure to work with, although the singing was a bit much at times!' He saw David on a number of occasions after he became famous, singing around the clubs of Hull: 'He nearly always came up for a chat after the show and never appeared too busy to speak to old friends and acquaintances.'

Another Hull man who worked with David in the cement yard was a drummer in his spare time. In Hull, even today, every second person you speak to seems to have a part-time job as an entertainer on the local club round. David's younger brother, Keith, is a long-distance lorry driver by day and a club singer at the weekends. The drummer writes: 'An artiste was needed for an angling club social at the White Lion in Lombard Street where I was playing and I offered the job to David. We had a very good night and his singing went down very well. He was reluctant to be paid for his efforts but I gave him ten shillings when the going rate at that time was 7/6d. Later, when David had made the grade and was one of the country's top singers, he invited all his workmates from Hull Concrete Stone Company for a night out at the Palace Theatre. We had a wonderful night. We lost touch when David started his singing career, but he never forgot us.'

In the few spare hours which he managed to get from his day-time job, mostly in the late evening, he sang. Steadily he began to make progress in his home town. He began by entertaining in the working men's clubs where so many of today's television stars began and gained their initial, priceless, experience. He was very popular and word soon got around among the club owners that a fine singer was available. Eventually he began to sing on a regular basis for £1, as much as he earned for a day's work at the cement yard. It must have been about then when David, still determined, despite failing to break into the professional singing ranks, had the confidence, or arrogance, to demand a performance fee of a guinea, according to one club owner. He always got it. It must have been

Brother Ted shaking hands with Shiela at the Whitfields' wedding

quite obvious to his boss at the yard when David had had a late night the day before, but he made every effort to encourage him in his show business career. In a radio interview many years later David recalled: 'Sometimes I had to take time off work, usually for an odd broadcast. The boss, Mr. Howden, always treated me very fairly and he always allowed me to go without asking any questions. I wasn't really satisfied with the progress of my singing career, though, and it seemed as though it was going to take an age to become a full-time singer, which is what I really wanted.'

On his return to civilian life David began going steady with Shiela Priestman, the home town girl he had met in his teens and written long letters to on his frequent trips abroad in the Navy. Letters from home, especially from girls, are an essential part of a sailor's life, even if there are girls in every port. They decided to get married, even though David's singing career had not yet reached the heights they had hoped for. The wedding took place on 9 June 1951 at St. Saviour's Church, Wilmington. It was a very quiet affair. Only Doris, as chief bridesmaid, and Ernie, the best man, attended from David's side of the family, although his elder sister Lily, who was heavily pregnant, went to the church. After the reception, at the Trocadero in Hepworth's Arcade, they caught a bus to Scarborough where they spent a quiet week's honeymoon.

'We stayed at a quiet little guest-house,' recalls Shiela. 'We had glorious weather and spent most of the time on the beach.' She even managed to stop David fulfilling any singing engagements for a whole week.

After the honeymoon, he went back to the old routine, his old job at the Hull Concrete Stone Company during the day, and singing at club concerts during the evenings and nights. He got quite down-hearted about his prospects of ever becoming a full-time singer and even considered the unthinkable: giving up the idea of becoming a professional singer.

Then, out of the blue, Hughie Green got in touch with him again. He wanted David to appear in a concert at the Criterion in London and added that it might lead to something bigger and more permanent. Once again he had to ask his boss for a couple of days off and once again it was granted.

The concert turned out to be for the benefit of the male employees of a well-known baby powder manufacturer, a sort of 1950's stag night, with none of the acts that are conjured up in the mind at the mention of 'stag night' now. David was very nervous, much preferring the more intimate atmosphere of the pubs and clubs of his native Hull. But, if he was to achieve his ambition of becoming a professional singing star, he knew he had to sing to much larger audiences. He began with his usual party piece, *Goodbye*, and there was little doubt about the audience's appreciation. He left the stage at the end of his act to rapturous applause. His first venture on to a London stage had been an instant success.

Hughie Green's promise about bigger and better things also came true, for, unknown to David, a local impresario, Cecil Landeau, was in the audience, and after the show offered him a contract singing at the Washington Hotel. The fee would be £10 a week with accommodation thrown in, not a princely sum, but, at least, he would be appearing before a wider audience with the distinct possibility of being really discovered by one of the big impresarios. Things were beginning to look better for David and Shiela. He was still known as the singing sailor but now, at last, he was beginning to make the grade in show business as a civilian.

In the middle of 1952 there was an added complication: an addition to the family, a son, Lance, was born on the 18 May. David and Shiela were forced, therefore, to make a big, difficult, decision. Should he stay at a hard but steady job in Hull, with extra income from his evening club concerts, or could he accept the temporary engagement in London with the outside chance that it might lead on to a full-time professional career? The latter choice would also mean that Shiela would have to give up her own job, for they did not want to be separated so early in their marriage. Not only that: the baby would have to be left in Hull with Shiela's parents. It was a very difficult choice to make, but eventually they decided to chance their luck and go to London, which, with hindsight, as far as

David's career was concerned, was the right decision. Shiela freely admits that she cried her eyes out when they left the comfort of her home town, friends and family, and especially the baby, and headed south to the unknown in London.

In January 1953 David began singing at the Washington Hotel for £10 per week. They lived in at the hotel and David's act began at midnight when he walked on to the floor and sang two or three songs while the showgirls changed their costumes. Living in a large hotel after the comfort of their small terraced house with Shiela's mother and father seemed cold and impersonal. They seemed totally lost when they first arrived. Although it was not as cold as in Hull, January is not a particularly good month to change surroundings, and, although they used to lie in during the mornings, because of David's late performance, there was still the rest of the day to cover.

When they first arrived they spent the days visiting all the usual tourist attractions, especially the free ones, for finances were still very tight. The early part of the evenings were usually spent at Dirty Dick's pub opposite the hotel as they couldn't afford the hotel bar's prices. David and Shiela would make a couple of drinks last for hours while he played his favourite games of darts and shove-halfpenny before returning to the hotel to perform in the cabaret.

The hotel staff were particularly kind and helpful. One lady in particular used to come in every evening to make corsages for the lady guests to wear to dinner and the cabaret show. Shiela got quite friendly with her but sadly could not afford a corsage. Nevertheless, the florist used to give her one, free of charge, every evening in time for David's twelve o'clock act. Things got slightly better as the first signs of Spring began to appear in the capital but they were still homesick and really began to wonder whether they had made the right decision.

It was not quite as bad for David because he had his singing to occupy his mind. The late evening was spent getting ready for his act and most mornings he got together with his musical director for rehearsals and the trial of new songs and arrangements. On the floor of the cabaret, the initial nervousness disappeared and the young singer soon had the vast majority of the audience with him. One thing that David found quite difficult at the beginning was singing to an audience who were eating at the same time as listening to his act. Even in the pubs of Portsmouth and the bars of Hong Kong an instant silence would come about when his rich tenor voice boomed out over the crowded room. This was not always the case at the Washington. One regular diner used to talk all the way through his act and never failed to clatter her cutlery while eating. Finally, his Yorkshire bluntness came to the fore, and he told the hotel manager that, unless the woman quietened down in the future, he would not go on with his act. We will never know whether this particular lady dined at another hotel or whether she ate earlier in the evening, but David got his way and she was not seen again. The Whitfield luck held out once more because, towards the end of his contract at the hotel, two guests dropped in to see his act. One was the Decca record company's talent scout, Bunny Lewis, and the other was the show business manager and publicity agent, Frederic Mullally. This time David had been forewarned that they were in the audience and he gave the performance of his life. At the end of the show the two business men got up and walked out without a word and a very disappointed David went to bed.

Chapter Seven

The First Recordings (1953)

In March 1953 the contract at the hotel finished and David and Shiela got ready to return to Hull. Many promising openings had looked likely but, unfortunately, none had materialised. They did not realise as they packed their bags for home that 1953 was going to be the year of the big break-through on the stage, but, more important to David's career, entry into the record charts. Just before they left London he received a call from Bunny Lewis asking him to make a test recording. David eagerly accepted, but just a test record was not enough. The recording industry was littered with the rejected discs of young hopefuls who had not quite made the grade. The representatives from the record company were very encouraging and optimistic, assuring David that he had the potential to become a big star. But words and half-promises did not help to pay the bills, so once again he returned to his old job in the cement yard. Shiela was disappointed, but more than glad to get home to her parents, infant son and the familiar surroundings of Hull.

They had only been back at home for a few weeks when Decca sent for David and he headed south once more to make his first record. With the backing of Nat Temple and his Orchestra he recorded *Marta* and *I'll Never Forget You*: both songs that he had performed successfully before live audiences for the past few years. *Marta*, in fact ,was a song from the early Thirties which had been introduced by Arthur Tracy, 'The Street Singer', and had even been recorded by the great Gigli. Neither achieved the eventual success of David with the song. *Marta* was played regularly on Jack Jackson's *Record Round-up* and various other disc jockey programmes while the agonising wait began to see if the record would sell. The advertising machine of the giant record company went into top gear and it and David's strong tenor voice played their individual parts. Within four weeks of the record's release it had sold over 20,000 copies. This was an excellent start for a first record from any unknown singer, especially one who was just about to give up all hope of a professional singing career.

After this things began to move very quickly. Bunny Lewis introduced David to publicity expert, Frederick Mullally, with whom he signed a personal management agreement, and another recording session was quickly arranged. Fred set about organising the aspiring star treatment of voice and dramatic training, constant rehearsals and recording sessions. He even insisted that David's hair was re-styled, his teeth fixed, and the ex-cement mixer's hands manicured, much to the singer's disgust. It was reported that the whole treatment cost the agent the princely sum of £205, but it was money well spent as his commission was 20% of David's earnings for the first few years and the singer was soon bringing in more than £500 a week. Shiela recalls going to London with David to meet Fred Mullally: 'I thought what a really nice man he was, and I was surprised that he lived in the splendour of Claridge's. It didn't dawn on me that it was a result of his agent's work and we and other artistes were paying.' To be fair, it worked both ways. Without this star treatment and expert guidance it would have been very difficult, if not impossible, for David to achieve the heights he did in such a short time in the mid-Fifties. Immediately after the success of his first record he was offered a week's Cine-Variety at the East Ham Granada: it was decision time again. After long discussions with Shiela, David decided to take the chance and return again to London, although this time he would be going on his own. Shiela was not prepared to leave her son, Lance, for any length of time again.

David went off to see his boss at the cement yard, telling him that he really thought that this time would turn out to be his big opportunity. 'It had better be,' said Mr Howden. 'I want to see you get on, but I don't think I can afford to give you another chance if you don't make good this time. I'll have to take on someone else.'

On 26 April 1953 David Whitfield stepped on to the stage to begin his full-time professional career and enter the spotlight where he was to remain for the next few years, before the advent of rock and roll pushed ballad singers

David visiting workmates, 1953

into the show business background. At last his dreams and ambitions were being realised and it looked as though the decision to leave Hull had been the right one.

The audience on that first night was packed with agents and impresarios waiting expectantly to hear this very promising newcomer. David recollected that night: 'I was scared stiff. The stage looked so big and awesome, as though I'd be swallowed up if I put a foot wrong. So much was at stake. I remembered that Vera Lynn had made her debut there. Could I hope to match her success?' He could and did in the next four years, reaching heights of international stardom that she never quite achieved. He was paid £75 for that week's work, quite a lot of money in 1953, when his tough, back-breaking job in the cement works had paid less than £10 a week.

Not only was his stage career taking off but his second record, *I Believe*, was selling even more than the first one. The sales ultimately reached 75,000 as it steadily climbed up the charts despite intense competition from the American singer, Frankie Laine. Even these sales were not enough to get into the Top Fifty in the record-buying Fifties and it was not until it was re-released seven years later that it just about crept into the chart reckonings. It seemed at last that Britain had a male singer who could compete with the best of the artistes from across the Atlantic and hold his own.

So what made David Whitfield the successful star that he became in 1953? At that time there really seemed to be two main routes to singing stardom. One was to become a singer with one of the big bands – most of the top American singers had taken this route. The other was to appear on the variety circuit and gradually move up to top billing. David, with his experience around the clubs and with Hughie Green's tour, virtually had the second option chosen for him, and this eventually led to top record sales, another absolute necessity on the way to singing stardom. It was a classic ' chicken and egg' situation: you sell more records and get more stage bookings, then more stage appearances lead to further record sales.

In 1953 the country was beginning to emerge from the aftermath and austerity of the war years. The younger generation had money to spend and a lot of that cash went on buying records. Above all, the population at large and, in particular, the agents, recording companies and impresarios were looking for a British singer, male or female, who would be popular enough to break the domination of performers from across the Atlantic. David Whitfield, blond and good looking, with a powerful voice and new style, was just what they wanted, and, with star grooming and media build-up, he became the most successful British international singer there had so far been.

Throughout 1953, as well as recording, David continued in variety, touring the country, and almost instantly achieving top billing. At the beginning of October his third recording, *Bridge of Sighs,* was Number Nine in the Top Ten for a week. He had finally made the big break-through. This was immediately followed by a record on a religious theme called *Answer Me*. It was selling steadily and well when what could have been a disaster turned out to be a blessing in disguise: the BBC banned it because of the lyrics. Instead of lessening the demand for the record, it had the opposite effect. It became the Number One request on Radio Luxembourg and in six weeks sold the amazing total of 700,000 copies. Once again, David was in competition with the American Frankie Laine, who started with the song as Number One, only to be toppled by David's version. This was his first Number One record and it held its position for 13 weeks. It is difficult to see through 1994 eyes what the controversy over the lyrics was about. The offending words were, 'Answer me, O Lord', when a boy lost his girl friend to someone else. The record was subsequently re-recorded with the words, 'Answer me, my love', which finally appeased the powers-to-be in the BBC. They must have been thoroughly peeved when they realised what a valuable piece of free advertising they had given to David in their anxiety to be correct.

A letter, published in the Catholic newspaper, *Universe*, at the end of 1953 gives an interesting sideline to the affair. It was written by Father George Long of the Kensal Catholic Youth Club, and read: ' I found the boys and girls listening with rapt attention to some records made by a new, and I'm told, very popular British singer called David Whitfield. One of his songs was a lovely ballad called *Answer Me*. It was a simple love song incorporating a plea for Divine intercession. Quite a change from the usual trash one hears on the average record. I feel there is a lesson in this. If a record "idol" like Whitfield can hold his fans among the youth without descending to the sub-moronic in his choice of songs, this must be an encouragement to the song-writers themselves to raise the standard of their lyrics. I think there is also a lesson for the BBC, who are perhaps more responsible than anyone else for the sales of records.'

With the increase in record sales, the Whitfield earnings soon began to climb into the £500 a week class. At the end of 1953 and the beginning of 1954 nearly every record issued was an instant hit, and numbers like *Rags to Riches, Bridge of Sighs* and *The Book* all edged into the Top Ten. According to the *Guinness Book of Hit Singles*, David Whitfield had more records in the charts during the Fifties than any other male British singer. He toured variety theatres up and down the country week after week and broke audience records wherever he went. The really hard work and early disappointments were now making it all worth while.

His biggest ovation was reserved for the Tivoli Theatre, Hull, in June. The theatre was packed to capacity and David was mobbed wherever he went during that week in his home town. This welcome must have

With Frankie Vaughan at the International Song Festival, Knokke-le-Zoute, Belgium

impressed him most of all, and made him realise that he had arrived in show business. He was now a star.

The following month he was chosen, with Frankie Vaughan, to represent Britain in the International Song Competition, a fore-runner of the Eurovision Song Contest, at Knokke-le-Zoute in Belgium. A clip from the *Hull Daily Mail* states: 'At the Casino in Knokke, David Whitfield won £150 for winning the event. Singers from France, Belgium, Holland and Luxembourg were competing on the second day of the European first festival of popular song. The award was for the best interpretation of any song sung by any artist. He won with his rendition of *I Believe*. A panel of judges representing all the competing countries gave him a unanimous verdict. He only started singing professionally three months ago and he is due to appear in Newcastle next Monday.' David also sang his new song, *Mardi Gras*, at this gathering, a song that was to be the 'B' side of *Rags to Riches* when it was released at the end of the year.

With the success of his variety performances and the sales of his records, David took on the mantle of super-star, a status usually only accorded to pop stars from across the Atlantic. He was mobbed outside theatres and recording studios and many of his fans, who still idolise him today, 14 years after his death, come from that era. A lady from Bognor writes: 'I first met him in May 1953 in Portsmouth, after seeing him sing at the Theatre Royal. I became one of his most faithful fans. I think I have all of his 78 records. I followed him around the country to his shows, spoke to him and had tea with him in Blackpool. I still have my scrapbook with cuttings and pictures signed by him.'

Other people became life-long fans because of an incident in their life involving David, who always seemed willing to appear for charity or to help people who were at a low ebb. Of course, it is easy to be cynical and say that, 'it's all good publicity for the star' – which is true – but David Whitfield seemed to take it one stage further. People who knew him felt that certainly in the Fifties he really cared. An up-to-date account from a young widow, with two young children in 1953, bears this out: 'I was in Raywell Sanatorium being nursed back to health from tuberculosis, which only a short time before had killed my husband. David had only just turned professional and I wrote asking if he would come and see us at Raywell. At the time he was topping the bill at the Tivoli (Hull). We had a matron who was a bit of a tartar and one day she asked me if I'd been writing to Mr. Whitfield, and I said I had. Matron said, "He's here." '

David went on to perform an impromptu sing-a-long in the male ward, which, incidentally, was definitely against his contract. Because the girl was sent back to her bed in the other ward, David sang outside her hospital window in the pouring rain. She was eventually cured and re-married but never forgot the kindness of the singing star.

Where did David's wife Shiela stand in all this teenage adulation? It was a rare thing in the Fifties and Sixties for pop stars even to admit they

David singing Cara Mia *to his fans*

44

were married, but David's fans seemed to accept it. Shiela agrees it was a bit of a strain: 'David used to get mobbed by his fans and I found that a strain as David did. I used to see the girls round David and think, "I don't know whether I like this or not." It took me a while to come to terms with it. But we got to know the girls and see them wherever we went and became quite friendly with them. I had to accept it as part of David's life. David was always terrific with his fans and never slid out of the back door to avoid them as some stars do. We could never eat until after the show, sometimes after midnight, but no matter how hungry we were David always had time for his fans.'

The year ended with David venturing into yet another facet of show business, that of pantomime, when he appeared in *Aladdin* at Bolton with Ben Wrigley and Bill Maynard. 1953 had turned out to be his most successful year to date and would have exceeded his wildest dreams at the beginning of the year. Little did he know that 1954 was going to be even better and the effects and world-wide sales of one record would raise him to international super-star status just over one year after turning professional.

Chapter Eight

Cara Mia (1954)

Although 1954 was probably the highlight year of David's life, it almost started with what could have been a tragedy, an abrupt ending to his career in show business and an end to his life. In late January of that year his car, with David driving and three passengers, skidded off an icy road near Elvington and finished up in a field. He had been appearing at the Empire Theatre in York and was returning to his home at Lorraine Street after the show. The subsequent newspaper report reads thus: 'After crashing against a telegraph pole, the car smashed its way through a hedge, and was completely wrecked. A passing motorist gave Mr. Whitfield and his passengers a lift into Hull.' None of them were injured apart from a few cuts and bruises. A very lucky escape indeed. David's younger sister, Doris, gives an even more graphic account of the accident: 'We remember the car crash very well, as he was bringing Walt (Doris's husband) back home. Walt was sitting in the front with David, and his father-in-law and friend, Sid Norris, were in the back. Walt had just said to David, "Mind this sharp left-hand bend, and, before they knew it, they had missed it and went straight through the hedge into a field. Walt and David were lucky, but Mr. Priestman and Sid were thrown out and hurt. It was only the next but one village to us, so they were nearly home. The car was a brand-new Vauxhall Velox. Next night when David called I had Walt's arm in a sling, pretending he'd broken his arm, but he soon caught on.'

By the beginning of this year David had become one of the biggest box office draws in the variety theatre. He was appearing further and further afield. During March he flew to Belfast for the Songwriters' Guild Concert, *Our Friends the Stars*, taking the whole orchestra and company of London's Victoria Theatre with him. He also appeared at Leeds, Glasgow and London during the same month. The schedule was very demanding and probably led to his throat troubles at the end of the month. In conjunction with his variety performances, all his records continued to reach the Hit Parade and in the early summer he made the record which was to be his biggest success of all, *Cara Mia*.

Even the introduction of this record had an element of luck in it. David and his musical director were searching for a new hit song ready for the summer season and, during a week at Dudley Hippodrome, just before it closed in May, Bunny Lewis sent David a new song that he insisted had all the makings of a hit. The letter from Bunny said, ' I will let you have a suggestion for the other side of the record in a day or two.' A few days later, the second number arrived and David takes up the story about the song that was to be his greatest hit: 'I was just having a shave in my dressing room in a theatre just outside Birmingham when my musical director, Reg Warburton, came in and said, "Listen to this."

' "I can't, I'm covered in lather," I replied, but he was so insistent I wiped my face and joined him in the other room. The song was beautiful, and I learnt it in just half an hour. Incidentally, the song for the other side of the record had taken me a week to learn. I knew the second song was going to be a Number One hit straight away and it was. It was *Cara Mia*. We even bet a rather sceptical Bunny Lewis that it would outshine the original side one and it certainly did.'

Cara Mia was first sung by David on 26 June at Blackpool, where he was appearing in the Summer Show. It brought the house down at every performance and was released on record on 1 July. The song fitted the Whitfield voice to perfection, and, anywhere in the world where the song is heard, the name of David Whitfield is immediately recalled, even years after his death. With a backing by Mantovani and his Orchestra, another surefire success in record sales at the time, the record far exceeded any prior expectations. By mid-June it was top of the Hit Parade, and before the end of that month had sold over 300,000 copies. It was to stay as Number One for nearly three months. Record shops sold out of their stocks and could not get fresh supplies quickly enough. Above all, it soon became a big success in the U.S.A. the first record by a male British singer to reach the American Top Ten. It eventually won David a gold disc for the sale of over 1,000,000 records, and by now has probably sold twice that number.

So, what made this song such a success? Admittedly, David was surging upward in popularity at the time, but most of his previous hits had a religious theme, which seemed to be the record company's gimmick of the time. It was possibly a combination of things which came together at just the right moment: David's voice, with the dramatic top 'C' at the end of the song, a note incidentally that he admitted he could not quite reach for radio and stage audiences in the future; the excellent backing of the Mantovani Orchestra; and, of course, the music written by Tulio Trapani, the pen name of Mantovani himself. Bunny Lewis, the Decca publicity man, actually wrote the words to the song so it was produced straight out of the recording company's family. One also must not forget the Decca

Company's image makers and publicity machine, but even they could not have conjured up such a big hit out of nothing.

Cara Mia proved to be the song that propelled David from being a new popular singer in Britain to one who was recognised all over the world. The song dominated the music trade during the summer of 1954, going around the world and being especially popular in Britain, the United States and Europe. He used it as his signature tune, and his new house in one of the smarter areas of Hull was subsequently named after it. The story goes, though it has not been substantiated, that even the toilet roll holder in the bathroom played the tune.

David's mode of travel also improved when he bought an enormous American car, a white Cadillac, on the proceeds from *Cara Mia*. The car was also named after the song and became the first of many of David's cars to bear the distinctive number plate, DW 100. The car cost £2000 and was described by one of his friends as, 'a space ship with a chromium mouth organ grinning across the front'.

One correspondent, who played with Lance when he was a boy, remembers driving down Commercial Road in Portsmouth in the car a few years later, with the hood down and David singing at the top of his voice, much to the embarrassment of his young passengers, and the surprise of the afternoon shoppers. The huge white car also proved irresistible to the bobby-soxed female fans who used to scrawl their

David and his white Cadillac

48

messages of undying love in lipstick on the sides. This was acceptable for a star, but scratched initials on the paintwork by using a nail file was really going too far. It once cost David £80 to have the car re-sprayed.

In one of his interviews at the time David recalled an evening when he went out to dinner with his old friend, Hughie Green. When he mentioned *Cara Mia,* Hughie winced. It appeared that Hughie, who once ferried aircraft for a living, was flying across the Atlantic one dark night when he needed a radio bearing. He switched on the receiver expecting to hear the required bearing when the voice of David Whitfield came through loud and clear, belting out his signature tune.

The second half of 1954 introduced David to the hectic rush that was the life-style of the top pop star, the seven-day working week. There was the round of theatres, personal appearances and all the other engagements on six days, and then travel to the next week's appointments on the seventh. He did the first of many Blackpool seasons during the summer but eventually managed to get away with Shiela for their first real holiday in Madeira.

October showed a slight blip in the over-all success story with a backstage battle that proved that the singer who had always shown a degree of arrogance and obstinancy, some would call it Yorkshire stolidness, was prepared to stand up to all around him if he considered it in his best interests. David was preparing for his appearance at the London Palladium, where he intended to sing Tolchard Evans' *Dance Gipsy, Dance*. He insisted that the accompanying orchestra should include strings: obviously the success of the Mantovani backing was fresh in his mind. After much high-level diplomacy the Jack Parnell Band was augmented by violins and cellos for rehearsals. David had got his way but it did lead to later accusations of big-headedness from certain fellow performers.

On 1 November, David, complete with *Cara Mia*, won rapturous applause at the 1954 Royal Variety Performance. In just over a year David had shot from comparative obscurity into the forefront of the world's top performers. From the clubs of Hull and the pubs of Portsmouth to appearing before Royalty at the London Palladium. At the Palladium that night David appeared with such international stars as Noel Coward, Bob Hope, Guy Mitchell, Howard Keel and his old adversary in song, Frankie Laine. After the show he was one of the 60 artistes to shake hands with the Queen. The boy from the back streets of Hull had come a long way. The Queen asked him how long he had been singing professionally?

'Eighteen months, ma'am', replied David.

'What were you doing before that?' she enquired.

David replied that he had served in the Royal Navy, and the Duke of Edinburgh, following along behind, asked him what ships he had served

H.M. The Queen speaking to David after the Royal Variety Show, 1 November, 1954

(l. to r.) Frankie Laine, Guy Mitchell, D. W., Dickie Valentine

on. David had got as far as the *Ramillies* when the Duke remarked, 'I was on there, 14 years ago.' The stage success story continued after the Royal Show with appearances at Sunderland, Edinburgh and Glasgow. He was due to appear at the Hippodrome, Birmingham, for a week but the punishing schedule of the previous two months had taken their toll and he was laid low with laryngitis. David Hughes stepped in to take his place and he was ordered to rest for a week. No doubt his forthcoming visit to America was also in his mind because he actually rested.

The successes of 1954 were not quite over. The year still had further surprises for David. Due to the great sale of *Cara Mia* in the U.S. and Canada, he was asked to appear on Ed Sullivan's *Toast of the Town* television show. His fellow artistes on this occasion were Sophie Tucker and the singing group, The Crew-cuts, and he was paid 4,000 dollars for singing just two songs. David flew to New York, all expenses paid, and on a Sunday in early December, his voice rested, he sang his two songs to millions of viewers. The reaction was amazing. After he had sung the songs, *Cara Mia* and *Santo Natale,* the television company's switchboard was jammed with calls from delighted Americans all anxious to pass on their congratulations.

This success on American television was all the more surprising because David was never as happy appearing before the television cameras as he was before a live theatre audience. He always said that singing to a camera lens was an artificial business that seemed to bring out more acting than singing ability. In any case, he had always thrived on his fans being in the audience to give him that boost to morale so desperately sought by entertainers. For all his outward confidence David, the perfectionist, was always very nervous before any performance right to the end of his career, and, according to Shiela, 'used to pace up and down behind the stage for a long time before his actual appearance.' The presence of a live audience and so many of his fans when he stepped out from the curtain always gave him that burst of adrenalin that carried him through his act.

The United States fell over itself to welcome the young British singer. On his arrival, a 12-hour press conference was arranged lasting from 12 noon until midnight and dozens of America's best known newspaper and television columnists and disc jockeys were present. Sixteen taped interviews were carried out during the course of the evening, each one lasting ten minutes. A contingent representing the David Whitfield American fan clubs turned up uninvited, and by the time the conference had ended over 300 guests had attended.

Later, during the short stay, David visited the El Morocco night club, a place whose front door he would not have been allowed to pass as a humble matelot on his previous visit to the U.S.A. during the war. Personalities he had only seen on the cinema screen, like Sonja Henie, James Stewart and Alfred Hitchcock, were introduced to him. It is also said that he had a long distance telephone conversation with Betty

On the Ed Sullivan Show: (l. to r.) Sophie Tucker, Ed Sullivan, D.W., Unknown.

Hutton, who had watched his performance on the Ed Sullivan Show. She invited him to her Hollywood home, but unfortunately time, in the form of a contract back in England, did not allow it.

After the visit he was asked by a reporter what he thought of America: 'I was very happy there but very tired. America can be a wonderful place, but so can London Airport when your wife is waiting to meet you there.'

David later appeared in six more Ed Sullivan shows, a record for any British performer before or since. After one of them the film producer, Joe Pasternak, expressed interest in his voice and asked him to contact him on his next visit. When he arrived home he mentioned it to a journalist who blew it up into a big story, saying that David was lined up to take over from Mario Lanza. This infuriated David, who had great regard for Lanza, and it intimated that he was doing some kind of deal behind the American tenor's back. Worst of all, following the Palladium incident, it again gave the impression of big-headedness: that David, who always tended to call a spade a spade, had ideas well above himself, or so it seemed to his show- business critics. A newspaper headline, just before Christmas 1954 said, 'Hollywood offers for David Whitfield.' It went on to mention 'a test for M.G.M. at Elstree in February and further screen tests in Hollywood for other film companies.' So 1954 ended on rather a sour note, a pity after all the good things that had happened during the year.

His old mentor, Hughie Green, was asked the reasons why David's flirtation with Hollywood and film stardom did not materialise and he

Singing Rudder and the Rock *on the Ed Sullivan Show*

gave two reasons. Firstly, his Yorkshire accent. It did not show when he was singing, but almost certainly David would have been involved in musicals, and leading men in those films had to do a great deal of talking as well. Fred Mullally had tried in vain to get him to take elocution lessons, 'electrocution' as David jokingly named them. He had started the course of voice tuition but refused to continue with it, and once he had made his mind up that was that. The second reason given for the Hollywood failure was the power of the stage and variety magnates in Britain in the Fifties. David was warned in no uncertain terms that if he stayed in Hollywood for any length of time, breaking his contract, then he would not be welcomed back to the British variety circuit and would find it very difficult to get any national bookings. There can be little doubt also, and this is echoed by Shiela, that David genuinely loved his country and home town, and would not have been willing to give them up.

Although the song *Cara Mia* must be considered the success story of 1954 and any other year, 1954 cannot be left without note of the other record successes of that year. At the beginning of the year, in January, *Answer Me* made a re-appearance at Number 12 in the Hit Parade for just one week. In March, *The Book* climbed to Number 5, disappeared and came back again in May at Number 10. But the second biggest hit of the year in Britain also did well in the U.S.A. *Santo Natale* reached Number 2 in the British Hit list during the Christmas period and on into the New Year.

The end of 1954 also coincided with a continuation of David's throat problems which were to trouble him throughout his singing career. Immediately after returning from the U.S.A. he was confined to bed to recuperate after another bout of laryngitis. He was told that he was not to sing again until he had rested completely. Nevertheless, he was happy to be home again, looking forward to Christmas shopping with Shiela and Lance, away from the hurly-burly of show business, followed by a holiday in Switzerland to complete his enforced rest.

In Switzerland, 22 January, 1955
(Picture courtesy Hull Daily Mail)

Chapter Nine

Everywhere (1955)

David and Shiela returned from his convalescence in Switzerland at the beginning of January. The short rest ordered by his doctor as a result of his throat problems at the end of 1954 had done him the world of good, and he was raring to return to the pantomime in Wolverhampton. One important lesson he had to learn as a professional singer was to pace himself, always a difficult task. There could be little doubt that his laryngitis and tonsillitis had been brought about by his hectic concert tours and the subsequent trip to America in the previous year, although it was a trip he could not afford to miss.

On 25 January he took over his role in *Aladdin* from Teddy Johnson, who had stepped in at the last minute on the opening night, and played David's part for three weeks. A review by George Bartram in a local newspaper greeted David's return thus: 'The tumultuous reception has grown louder every night at the Grand, Wolverhampton, yet this has not affected the off-stage manner of David Whitfield. David is literally rocking the town with his 30-minute spot in *Aladdin* and Wolverhampton will undoubtedly be a quieter town after the final show. Whitfield, the fabulous, likes to mix with ordinary folks; slip across the road from the theatre to the Greyhound pub any night and there you will find David and his conductor, Reg Warburton, challenging all comers to a game of darts. These two are champs and the landlord knows it. Business is certainly brisk when the two "W's" are fighting it out, and they like nothing better than to play anyone willing for a game.' The reviewer was obviously a Whitfield fan but it was certainly true of David at this time, and for most of his life, that he was happier being just one of the boys. The question was, as world stardom beckoned, could he continue to be? It was certainly easier in the Fifties than later, when the advent of rock and roll introduced the squealing masses that forced the rock stars to be heavily body-guarded, but it still had its problems for someone who had recently been catapulted into public stardom. A lot of the teen-age adoration that until

In Aladdin, *Grand Theatre, Wolverhampton, 1955*

then had been reserved for the transatlantic stars was now being directed at David.

What is true is that right to the end of his career David preferred staying with friends rather than in hotels, and he always seemed to form long-lasting relationships with pub landlords and café owners in premises adjacent to the theatres where he performed. This obviously left him very accessible to fans. Several of the female ones who hung around his digs and the theatre after the show hoped for more than just to hear their hero sing or get his autograph.

The grinding work schedule continued in 1955 because, in addition to the pantomime, Sunday, which should have been the rest day, usually ended in a one-night performance in a nearby town. For instance, the first Sunday after returning to the panto David appeared at the De Montfort Hall in Leicester, billed as 'Britain's Sensational Top Singing Star'.

His business arrangements also changed at the beginning of the year when Lew and Leslie Grade took over complete management control from Fred Mullally. That was not the only change: Bunny Lewis resigned from Decca in the summer, leaving David to carry on recording without the man who had first introduced him to the record company. By this time David could be considered a seasoned entertainer but he was still a comparative novice when it came to dealing with the politics and manoeuvres of show business. He first met another Humberside star, Ronnie Hilton, who was on his way to stardom, at about this time and gave him some very valuable advice.

'You've had more experience at this game than me. How do you cope with all the new friends who suddenly want to know you?' asked Ronnie.

'Act dumb,' David told him. 'Learn as much as you can about show business as well as singing, but never let the other dressing rooms know you are learning. You'll find there are plenty of "friends" who want to slap your back with a knife in their hands. The more green they think you are, the better you'll be able to manage them.'

David improved his position in the *Melody Maker* poll, moving from 12th in the previous year to 5th in 1955 in the best male singer category.

The hit record band-waggon also continued, the four discs that were issued in this year all appearing in the Top Twenty and remaining there for several weeks. *Beyond the Stars* reached Number Eight in February, *Mama* was 12th, and in and out of the charts in May, June and July, *When You Lose the One You Love* was 7th in November in Britain, and, surprisingly enough, the top-selling record in Chicago. His biggest hit of 1955, *Everywhere*, was Number Three for 20 weeks starting in July. The last two named recordings are considered by many Whitfield fans as the best he ever did, including *Cara Mia*. He never had another Number One after *Cara Mia* but the records released at this period always sold enough to keep him in his place as Britain's top male recording star.

David was also taking the opportunity to widen his horizons. He had already appeared in America and on the Continent, and a further country was added by a trip to the home of the tenor, Ireland. He had met the Irish singer, Josef Locke, on his circuits of the music halls and variety theatres and, because Josef was nearly ten years older, it was a standing joke between them that David always called him 'Dad'.

He appeared at the Theatre Royal, Dublin, in April after a show in Belfast. This time he was mobbed by crowds who broke through the police cordon at the railway station. Fame was beginning to have its drawbacks, but David could not and did not complain. These were the people who were buying his records by the thousands. April also saw David and Reg Warburton make a second visit to New York for several personal appearances in the City, and another session on the Ed Sullivan Show. Two of Tolchard Evans' songs, *Everywhere* and *Lady of Madrid*, were David's stock numbers in his American radio and television shows and it was interesting that the Welsh composer was at London Airport to meet him on his return. The return was marred slightly by an interview with a journalist who implied afterwards that David's frequent trips to the U.S.A. had gone to his head.

David started the summer season at the Winter Gardens in Blackpool, still with the over-arrogance criticism in the air which rather upset him, especially as he had been looking forward to the show and as Shiela and Lance had taken over a house in Blackpool for the season. The criticism was bad enough to swing his publicity men into action and led to David taking the opportunity to hit back at his critics when the following article appeared in a variety magazine. He wrote: 'It seems the more success you have the more difficult it becomes to be yourself. My story is well known. A couple of years ago I worked with my hands loading concrete slabs onto lorries back home in Hull. Then my voice changed my fortunes. But, and this is important, it didn't change me and neither has the success and the financial rewards that have come to me. Apparently this is all wrong. I still speak with the accent of a son of Hull; I still say what I think because I believe that honesty is worth more than well-chosen but insincere words. In show business circles, that's simply asking for it. They say that I'm conceited, so I'm big-headed because I haven't been influenced by every wise guy around.

'I have a high opinion of myself because I prefer to remain David Whitfield instead of copying the current way of life. Anyone really close to me would laugh at this and those who are near to me, my wife, Shiela, and my musical director, Reg Warburton, would be the first to take me down if I showed any real sign of big-headedness. True, I enjoy singing and I would be a fool if I didn't get a kick out of my career. When I'm singing well I'm inclined to bubble over with exhilaration. I suppose this can easily be mistaken for conceit. But there's another side to that picture. There are times when I get back to my dressing-room in the mood to kick myself, if I fancy I haven't given a good performance. And, believe me, Reg Warburton doesn't mince words if he feels that I've not been at my best. I get the old-fashioned bawling out, because Reg, like me, reckons that it's better to deal with facts than soft words. That's the kind of diplomacy we both understand.' David went on to say, 'My wife and I regard ourselves as ordinary people who have been blessed with good luck. I always had something of a voice. But I realise some good singers never get a break. I got one and happened to make good. When we are in Hull we love to drop in at the local working men's clubs where I did my early singing. And we are still, at the moment, living with Shiela's parents next to the concrete factory where I once worked.

'We are having our own house built because with one youngster we need the extra room – and because we can now afford it. There was a bit of a rumpus too about the possibility that I might make a film in Hollywood. When I appeared on one American TV show one of the important people I met was film producer, Joe Pasternak, who professed to like my voice and urged me to get in touch with him when I go to Las Vegas. The idea was that I should make a film test with a view to signing a contract. And that, in Mr Pasternak's view, would be a mere formality. I happened to mention this to a journalist when I got back and the story

was blown up really big. I was, according to the headlines, taking over where Mario Lanza left off. In fact, to judge by one story, I already regarded myself as a film star . . . ROT!

'I was the first to point out that I hadn't actually taken the test, and in any case, I'm not worried whether I go to Hollywood or not.'

David finishes the article by saying: 'No, I don't think I am big-headed, but I am, I suppose, forthright. I can't help it, it's my native Yorkshire inheritance and this I hope I never lose.'

The article seemed to quieten things down although it did leave him with one or two dangerous enemies in the press. It is possible that David's natural exuberance and excitement took over on his return from the U.S.A. and this was taken as a criticism of show business in this country where he had received his first chances.

The show business atmosphere was not always bad. At the beginning of September he was presented with a gold disc for the sale of the millionth copy of his record, *Cara Mia*. The ceremony was carried out at his fan club convention at the Winter Gardens, Blackpool, the presentation being made by Joan Regan during the afternoon. The ceremony was not without some anxiety for it was discovered at the last minute that the golden disc was missing. It transpired that it had been placed under the stage for safety and one of the organisers, seeing it there, had moved it. It was eventually found with just seconds to go before the presentation.

The *Melody Maker* reported on the event, saying: 'When David Whitfield staged a fan convention at Blackpool's Winter Gardens, his supporters rose to the occasion in magnificent style. Nearly, 2,000 fans, mostly teenaged girls, travelled by land, sea and air from as far as Ireland to sweep David off his feet and almost carry him onto the platform with hair, tie and clothes awry. The high spot of the afternoon was the presentation by Joan Regan on behalf of Decca Records of a golden disc to celebrate the sale of a million records of *Cara Mia*. The biggest cheer of the day came when, after receiving the award, David hugged his wife, Shiela.'

He was not the first British performer to receive a gold disc. Two other artistes, Vera Lynn and Eddie Calvert, had already beaten him to it but he was certainly the first British male vocalist to receive the award.

David's public engagements continued towards the end of 1955. He was always concerned deeply with charity causes and in September he arranged to visit one of the 108 Doctor Barnado Homes with fellow stars Alma Cogan, Ronnie Hilton and Dickie Valentine, the year being the centenary of the Homes. The end of the month saw him as one of the guests at the Savoy Hotel in London to help those old troupers, Wilfred and Mabel Pickles, celebrate their Silver Wedding Anniversary.

The radio and television work continued, although his television appearances were few and far between. He made a rare appearance on British television in November when he appeared in the *Daily Mirror's* Television Disc Festival at the London Palladium. According to close friends of David, his excuse for the infrequency of his television appearances was, 'I spend a week rehearsing in a TV studio for an hour show and only get paid for that one hour. I can earn four times as much in a week by touring.' No doubt the Yorkshire carefulness had something to do with it, but it is also possible that his outspoken criticism and poor comparison of British TV with that in the U.S.A. also played a part.

His radio work was much more frequent, especially as a lot of the radio shows were pre-recorded before invited audiences around the country: back to David's preference for appearing before a live audience. Most of the radio work was performed for Radio Luxembourg where David starred in the most expensive series ever put on the air by the station.

Regular flights to the United States carried on, with several dates on the Ed Sullivan Show, the programme that went out to 50 million viewers. Just consider how

At the Daily Mirror*'s Television Disc Festival, 1955*

many theatre audiences that would have covered. In October 1955, Shiela accompanied him for the first time on one of his trips across the Atlantic.

David was certainly moving in the right circles on these trips abroad. At a party to mark the première of the film *Guys and Dolls*, he met Esther Williams, Marlon Brando, Jean Simmons and Richard Egan – not bad connections for the ex-matelot and concrete carrier. It was on his return from this trip that he praised the cooperation received from the orchestras and accompaniments provided for his TV shows and cabaret acts while on tour in the USA. This remark again did not endear him to the British show business media and management.

The very successful year of 1955 came to an end with a week at the Hippodrome, Birmingham, followed by another week in Newcastle. No pantomime was forthcoming at Christmas and this gave David the opportunity to spend the holiday back with his family in Hull.

Chapter Ten

My September Love **(1956)**

During the first three months of 1956 David was kept busy with weekly bookings and one night stands up and down the country. He had now settled down into a regular touring routine and, although it was strenuous and tiring, he was learning to pace himself and leave time for regular visits to his family in Hull.

His big hit of this year was the song, *My September Love*, which first entered the charts in March at around the 18th position and then soared to Number 3 in April, holding that position for 20 weeks. The song made a brief return in September, of course, and became one of the most requested songs in his concert repertoire. The other two hits of that year were *My Son John* and *My Unfinished Symphony*, neither of which reached the heights of some of his biggest hits. Meanwhile, the rock and roll band-waggon was moving relentlessly on, so David, with his ballads, was doing very well to be in the charts at all.

In June he again took part in one of his regular charity concerts as one of the artistes who recorded songs for the Lord Taverners' record, *All Star Hit Parade*. The novelty of this recording propelled it into Number 3 in the Hit Parade within two weeks of its release. The proceeds went to charity so David did not make any money out of it, but the publicity value was important. He sang *It's Almost Tomorrow*, the Number One hit of the American group, 'The Dreamweavers'.

During the next month he made his second annual appearance in the *Daily Mirror* Disc festival; this was televised from the *Sunday Night at Blackpool* show. David was accompanied by many of the top bands and orchestras at this time, and on this occasion it was Geraldo and his Orchestra. The show was transmitted nationally over most of the ITV networks, another important facet in David's effort to stay in his position as Britain's top male recording star. Blackpool was one of David's favourite performance towns. After appearing in the last two years' summer shows, he was always assured of a welcome. His popularity was very evident when he returned for his first public concert of the year, appearing with Lita Roza and Ronnie Carroll at the Opera House and playing to record audiences. After Blackpool, he carried on with the touring, appearing during the summer months at the Empire, Leeds, the Hippodrome, Bristol and the Empire Theatres in Newcastle and Glasgow. There seemed to be a change in show business tactics here. After the rather settling influence of a seaside summer show for the season, the change seemed to be towards weekly stints in the main towns during the summer. No doubt it was possible to appear before more members of the record-buying public this way and perhaps it was also more lucrative. It had the effect of increasing his ever-growing fan clubs, an essential part of a successful pop singer's career. In 1954 the membership of the David Whitfield fan clubs stood at 1,500 but by 1956 it had risen to over 7,000. Hundreds of these fans followed David and his shows around the country. They have never forgotten him and, even now, when most have assumed a grandmother role, they still talk and write about him with very fond memories.

A lady wrote from Portsmouth: 'I am now a 51-year-old happily married lady with two grown-up wonderful sons. All those years ago, he made a shy, unhappy girl of 16 feel like a queen. He was a top star, Britain's Number One singer, yet he had time for me, and always remembered me. Although I know he did the same for many others, he was special for me.'

Many people have written about him, men and women, and their memories of happy days in the Fifties, and, although they were obviously biased, as avid fans usually are, the message always seemed to be that he took the time to make sure that his fans came first. Some of this could be put down to natural friendliness, but also David was a pretty astute performer and he knew a lot of the people who eagerly bought his records in the mid-Fifties could easily change their allegiance to another star literally over night. He said in an interview: 'Whenever people scoff at all the young fans who often besiege me at the stage door, I quickly jump on the side of the fans. They are the people who put me where I am today. So long as I can please these youngsters by signing their autograph albums, or handing out a few pictures, then I'm happy.' Sometimes, unfortunately, this loyalty to his fans came before his duty to his wife and family.

Another female fan from Fareham remembers: 'My friend and I travelled for years to see him, two shows a night for a fortnight. We also won a contest in a musical paper, *The Disc*, as being the most faithful fans of a pop star. Over the years he became a great personal friend and we had some really good times socially. I still have every record he made even the old 78's, still in original covers and all autographed. My husband and son can't understand why I keep all this stuff and are always taking the "mickey", but it's my youth and my memories of a wonderful period of my life.'

Most of the press criticism about David's film ambitions had died down in 1956 and he settled down to an enjoyable, and quite lucrative time in his show business career. He returned to variety, always his first love, for a season at the Prince of Wales Theatre in London in September, appearing with Joan Regan and Sid Millward. Unfortunately, at this show a report was written by a critic who it appeared did not belong to the David Whitfield fan club. He watched the show and had this to say about David's performance: 'Whitfield was a disappointment. Possessed of a pleasant enough voice, he sang sharp throughout the latter half of his programme. He strode around the stage like a boxer looking for a fight, while mouthing vowels with such exaggeration I was afraid he might swallow the pit orchestra. Perhaps I am jaundiced, though, for I must report that he undoubtedly received the loudest and most prolonged applause of the evening. One very pleasing aspect of his act – he didn't mention his recording once.'

It is possible that David had been receiving his 'electrocution' lessons just prior to the show and had gone over the top a little. In one of his radio interviews towards the end of his career he told a story about going into a large London store to buy a 'bath' paddling pool, as a surprise present for Lance. He decided to try out his newly acquired Oxford accent on the shop assistant and the Londoner could not understand what he wanted until he returned to his native Yorkshire accent. This, according to David, was the point where he flatly refused to continue with any more sessions to improve his diction.

This was not to say that he did not appreciate the voice lessons given to him by Professor Cunneli. At the beginning of his career he thought it was possible just to walk on to the stage and sing as he had done for years around the pubs and clubs. The control and discipline needed for hours of variety stage and recording studio rehearsals soon made him change his mind. In the same interview he gives a vivid impression of the famous professor's technique: 'After I had to appear twice nightly on the stage for 35 minutes and also rehearse in the mornings for hours I realised I needed some form of voice training. I went to see this Professor Cunneli, I think he was Polish, and he'd trained Rex Harrison, Alma Cogan and Yana.

'He was marvellous. If I had a recording session at ten in the morning and had had a rough night, I'd pop into his office first for five minutes and he'd have me singing like a lark at that time in the morning. Just by using techniques like singing through the scales with your tongue out. You used to feel like a right idiot, but it worked.'

In return, David was once described by the Professor as having ' the biggest pair of vocal chords I've ever seen, the heart of a lion and a chest like a bull'.

Of course, David's booming voice and singing did not appeal to everyone. Years after his death, Jean Metcalfe the BBC announcer, was asked about David Whitfield songs being constantly requested on *Forces* and *Family Favourites* programmes. She admitted that she could not stand David's voice and used to cringe if one of his songs was requested. She hastened to add that it did not bias her in any way against playing his records.

Although David did not visit the U.S.A. in 1956, nevertheless his records were selling well and there was still a lot of public interest in his singing. A magazine report from September read: 'David Whitfield is in line for a return appearance on Ed Sullivan's TV show in the States. Sidney Grace of the Lew and Leslie Grade office says, "David's records are selling in thousands in the States and Ed Sullivan is interested in having him back on his programme." '

As the year drew to an end David kept up his habit of appearing with different orchestras, as befits a star, although his partnership with Mantovani seemed to be at an end. It had been an excellent combination and had worked well for both of them as far as hit records were concerned. John Hanson, who also worked with Mantovani during this period, said in his book: 'I wish Monty (Mantovani) had written *Cara Mia* for me, instead of David Whitfield.'

David recorded a programme with Ronnie Aldrich and the Squadronnaires for Radio Luxembourg in October and, although he did not actually sing for once, he renewed his acquaintance with Alyn Ainsworth, conductor of the BBC Northern Dance Orchestra when he dropped into the Queen's, Blackpool, to congratulate him on his engagement to one of the Beverley Sisters.

On a more personal note, the *Melody Maker* of 20 October 1956 reported: 'David Whitfield may be the father of twins in March. He said last night, "My wife is just awaiting the results of the x-rays."' The magazine report turned out to be a false alarm, although it was partly right. The Whitfield's second son, Shane, was born in February of the next year.

It was in the Autumn of 1956 that David, Shiela and Lance, now four-years-old, moved from the terraced house in Stoneferry which they shared with Shiela's mother and father to a rather elegant nine-roomed house in Kirkella. Like all young married couples they had set their minds on eventually living on their own, and had looked at some three-bedroomed semis in the Garden Village in East Hull, when David had started his singing career after leaving the Navy. By 1956, money was not a problem, his frequent appearances in a variety of show business circuits, allied to the phenomenal record successes of the mid-Fifties,

Shiela, David and Lance in front of Cara Mia

(Picture courtesy Hull Daily Mail)

moved the Whitfields into the well-off class. Nearly all his business transactions were handled by his managers and agents, but they could almost afford anything as far as houses, cars and general comforts were concerned.

The red and green painted, newly built house was called *Cara Mia* – what else? – and some of the family's happiest moments were spent there. Features included a curved staircase leading up to four bedrooms, with a sun balcony outside the main bedroom. With the prospect of an even bigger family in the near future there was an upstairs playroom for the children.

George Roberts, a friend of David's old boss at the cement yard, was the architect for the new house. He still lives in Hull and remembers vividly the building and subsequent furnishing of *Cara Mia*: 'I was the architect responsible for the detail working drawings and supervision of works including furniture, soft furnishings and landscape gardening. I had no financial dealings with David, as architects' certificates of interim value surveys were sent direct to his agents, Lew and Leslie Grade, in Regent Street, London and the cheques for the contractors returned in payment. I did, however, spend a great deal of time with David and Shiela as clients, discussing in detail and advising on the design and equipment of *Cara Mia*. David was always very charming and completely unassuming in his attitude to everyone. He gave me a free hand as far as costs were concerned so that *Cara Mia* evolved as a building of text-book construction and specification of the highest quality materials and workmanship, ensured by daily supervision. The house was somewhat larger than usual, as it included accommodation for the Priestmans, Shiela's parents.

The distinguishing features which made it *Cara Mia* were the raised dais for the grand piano, over which was a curved wrought-iron screen formed of music rulings with the notes attached of the first few bars of the song. There were two sheet-metal records built into the front wrought-iron gates and the electric musical door chimes, also playing – guess what? All these features have, I am informed, been removed by one of the subsequent owners.

'I can remember one or two amusing incidents that reflect the real David Whitfield. Shortly after they moved in, I saw David planting small shrubs alongside the entrance drive. He was using a solid silver tablespoon as a trowel. I bent down to him and said, "Snob!" He replied with a smile, "So what, I can afford it." 'Also, while discussing the specifications, I was talking about furniture with David and Shiela and he informed me that she particularly insisted on a liver-shaped dressing table for the bedroom. You can work out that one for yourself!'

It was not surprising that one of the subsequent owners removed all evidence of *Cara Mia* from the house. It was rather like a place of pilgrimage for David's fans throughout the years and Shiela remembers young fans camping out on the grass island in the middle of the road in the late Fifties. After they left the house in 1971, fans still arrived in the road outside to gaze at the house and its surroundings. In fact, they still do.

There was a big disappointment for David in November when the Royal Variety Performance at the London Palladium was cancelled due to the war situation in the Suez area. A number of service reservists were called up for this crisis and David probably had visions of being kitted out once more in bell bottoms and a little round hat. David and Shiela had made an early return from their post-summer holiday to get back in time for rehearsals for the show. The rehearsals went ahead, but the show was cancelled at the last minute.

December started with a week's variety at the Finsbury Park Empire and a charity show for the Hungarian Relief Fund at the London Coliseum. David appeared with Eve Boswell, Alma Cogan, Shani Wallis, Norman Wisdom and the Geraldo Orchestra. The year ended rather sadly as David and his musical advisor, Reg Warburton, parted company after being together for the four years that David had been a professional. Reg was tired of the constant travel of musical director and accompanist to a top star and he settled for a job as a manager in his own office in London. There was no acrimony, unusual for show business break-ups, and they both kept in touch until David's death in 1980. This contact was made easier due to the fact that Reg managed Joan Regan, one of David's frequent fellow artistes on the theatre circuit around the country. David and Reg left the country on 29 December for Brussels as David was playing a week's engagement at L'Ancienne Belgique in Antwerp. This was followed by their final appearance together for a week in variety at the Regal Cinema, Hull, a fitting finale. Perhaps, during that week, David thought back to that evening years before when, as a young matelot, he had taken Shiela to that same building, then only a cinema, on their first date. Shiela was obviously in the audience in 1956, but neither could have dreamt in 1944 that he would be back, not as a member of the audience, but as a world star.

Ironwork in Cara Mia

(Picture courtesy Hull Daily Mail)

Chapter Eleven

I'll Find You (1957)

Paul Conrad joined David as his musical director at the beginning of 1957. The rather easy-going routine that he had had with Reg Warburton was changed, and David was kept up to scratch with Paul's insistence on a regular daily routine, a bit like a boxer in training. They met every morning at 11 o'clock in the theatre, or wherever David was performing, to practise scales and exercises, and to try out new songs. Paul felt, quite rightly, that voice training was just as important to a singer as physical training is to a sportsman. Not that the physical aspect was disregarded, fitness being very important because of the arduous tours and twice a night performances. They worked well together and Paul was obviously a very gifted musical director, but it was at this point that David's recording successes seemed to be fading away.

The year started very well with the song, *The Adoration Waltz,* entering the Hit Parade at Number 15 at the end of January, going up to Number 9, and then going out of the Top Twenty by the end of March. This was David's last recording venture into the Top Ten, although later in the year *I'll Find You* (1957) reached Number 27 and 28 in April and May respectively. It was written as the theme music for the film, *Sea Wife,* which was the first American film to have the music written by a British song-writing team and the theme song sung behind the credits by a top British singer. It was written by Tolchard Evans and Richard Mullan, and David had to race from one half of England to the other to fulfil the commitments necessary for recording this song. After appearing at Wolverhampton, he arrived in London at five in the morning; at ten o'clock he was in the studio and did seven takes with Muir Mathieson and the Philharmonia Orchestra. By two o'clock that afternoon he was heading north on his way back to Hull to see his family, now swelled to one more, with the birth of his second son, Shane, on 23 February. In his anxiety to get home he over-did the pressure on the accelerator and was booked for speeding. Obviously, the traffic policeman was not a Whitfield fan, unlike the one who once waved down a line of cars, including one carrying the operetta singer, John Hanson. He peered into the car, looked at John and then waved him through saying: 'We can't keep Mr. Whitfield waiting, can we?'

Although the film *Sea Wife* was made in the U.S.A., it starred an eminent British actor and actress, Richard Burton and Joan Collins. After the early Hollywood discussions and promises this was the nearest that David got to appearing in a film. Having said that, many people classify *I'll Find You* as one of the best songs that David recorded. Unfortunately the record-buyers did not quite agree. David had already recorded the song for the British market with the Roland Shaw Orchestra but it never achieved the success it deserved.

Many people have their favourite stories of David Whitfield and his thoughtfulness, but the beginning of 1957 cannot be left without mention of a 14-year-old schoolboy from Hull who had to spend a lot of his time in hospital with kidney trouble. David was his idol, he read magazine articles about the star, followed his fan club articles, bought all his records, and for him no other singer existed. Before very long everyone at Hull Royal Infirmary knew of the boy's admiration and David, who was appearing at the Regal in Hull, was invited to the hospital. He willingly accepted the invitation, despite a hectic theatre schedule, and spent half an hour talking to the boy at his bedside. The boy eventually made a good recovery from his illness and never forgot the singer's kindness. Many top artistes visit hospitals and participate in charity work but for David it seemed more than a publicity stunt and he genuinely felt an obligation, because of his own good fortune, to make some kind of repayment. He often said this in interviews and it was felt, even by his critics, that he really meant it.

David's tours of the country continued, with performances at Gaumont cinemas accompanied by many stars, including Ruby Murray and Penny Nicholas. He also held on to his star billing, as a poster for a one-night performance at Leicester testifies: 'Arthur Kimbrell presents the Number One Singing Star, David Whitfield, with Frank Weir and his Orchestra'.

In April David was among other show business guests of honour at a luncheon given by the Variety Club of Great Britain. The gathering was to honour gold disc winners and David said afterwards that even the menus were disc-shaped with gold lettering. The other gold disc artistes there were Winifred Atwell, Vera Lynn, Eddie Calvert, and his old accompanist, Mantovani, all of whom had achieved gold disc status during the Fifties.

Early May brought a much needed break and holiday for the Whitfield family in Italy. David was booked for a three-week tour of the army bases in Germany during May but found it impossible to fit it in between the holiday and a prior booked engagement in Newcastle, and the army tour

Attending a luncheon given by the Variety Club of Great Britain to honour gold disc winners, April, 1957

had to be cancelled. It appeared, in this instance, that David considered the family, and especially Shiela and the new baby, before his professional commitments.

The Newcastle show, *Five Past Eight*, started in June, with David performing for three weeks. The managing director of the show wrote in the local newspaper, 'I would like to contract Whitfield for the full season, but unfortunately he is booked elsewhere for the summer.'

The first signs of a slight shift from ballads to light operatic songs was evident in this show as a local reporter wrote: 'It is a David Whitfield with a difference who appears in the new, bright and breezy summer season show, *Five Past Eight*, at Newcastle's Theatre Royal. He now includes opera in his vocal offering and, judging by the popularity of his reception in this experiment, it looks as though he could do it with assured success.' Whether this was David's decision or that of his musical director is not known, but with hindsight he would probably have been better off sticking to the ballad type music that had made him famous. But he was never one to dodge a new opening, and he probably saw light opera as a fresh challenge.

The summer show mentioned by the Newcastle director was at the King's Theatre, Southsea. It was due to last for ten weeks and it started on 8 July. David returned to his old naval stamping ground near Portsmouth and only a mile or so down the road from his original talent show discovery just seven years before. A lot had happened in that time: he had shot to international success and achieved the position of British Number-One male singing star. Now, unfortunately, in some ways the signs were already there of a slight decrease in popularity, certainly as far as record sales were concerned.

A newspaper article, prior to the opening of the show, reported: 'Famous Decca vocal star, David Whitfield, has signed to play his first resident summer season in the South of England. From Monday, July 8th, he stars in a Bernard Delfont production – at the King's Theatre, Southsea – for a minimum of ten weeks. David's engagement was booked by Lew and Leslie Grade. Other musical personalities will be taking part, although the title of this presentation has yet to be decided. Supporting artists include Decca vocalist Audrey Jeans, besides clever instrumental trio, The King Brothers (who recently signed for the Parlophone label).

'Although David Whitfield scored a big success in Blackpool (for two successive seasons in 1954 and 1955), this Southsea venture will be his first long-term stay on the south coast.

'Prior to opening at Southsea, David will take two or three weeks holiday but in the immediate future his variety dates include Coventry Theatre (April 29th) and Rialto, York (May 6th).'

The show ended a very successful season on 15 September and it is interesting to note that this was the summer show where Harry Worth and Billy Dainty first appeared; both artistes soon to be famous in their own right.(It was also the one instance where the writer saw David Whitfield appear on the stage. I was serving in the Royal Navy at the time and took my mother and father to see the show as a treat for their silver wedding anniversary.)

Because of the long duration of the show David was able to be joined by Shiela and the two boys for the summer. As far as the weather was concerned it was not really suitable for the beach, but at least they were together. The family stayed at a large house, at 32, Turret Lodge, in Havant Road, Emsworth, a few miles along the coast from Portsmouth. Mrs. Sorrell, who still lives in Emsworth, writes: 'I was only a small child at the time and used to play with David Whitfield's son Lance in the garden. If my memory serves me right, I think they had only just had a baby. My friends and I, who played in the garden, had to rescue Lance one day when he slipped into the pond, although he was unhurt. Being only children we could never understand what all the fuss was about with the Whitfields, but my own mother was a big fan of his. So it really made her day when he gave some of us free tickets to see his show, but I'll always remember him when he knelt down in front of us and sang *Cara Mia*.'

The summer season was yet another success, with packed houses most

David, Shiela and Lance at Emsworth, near Portsmouth, 1957

nights, almost on a par with Blackpool. One of David's then young teenage fans also remembers that summer, and speaks for the hundreds of girls who used to hero-worship him: 'I met David in July 1957 at the stage door of the King's Theatre. David was appearing in a summer show, *Light Up The Town*, a very successful show playing to packed houses every night. I waited in a long queue outside the stage door for his autograph, I was 16, and suddenly before me was David, with his handsome face, giving me a beautiful smile, his blue eyes were sparkling, his golden hair was shining and he seemed to have a gold light all around him. That was my first impression of David, and I have never forgotten it. He used to sit in the cubby-hole by the stage door after each show and sign autographs, no matter how long the queue. He would always chat and laugh and joke with everybody, he had a lively, sparkling personality and he certainly lit up the town of Portsmouth when he was there.'

The fact that he liked to slip out between shows, 'to play darts and have a couple of pints', as the publicity men liked to say, was confirmed in real life by the same correspondent: 'David would walk a few yards up the road during the first half of the show, when he wasn't appearing, to play darts in a public house called The Lord John Russell. He would then return to the theatre, relaxed and happy, and get ready for his appearance as top of the bill, at the end of the show.'

The top of the bill act would usually perform for about 30 minutes but sometimes with several encores it could stretch to almost an hour. The ex-teenage girl's memories of his stage performances were: 'He would wear a black dress suit with bow tie, or a red silvery sparkling jacket with black trousers, or a white jacket with black trousers, always with a white dress shirt and black shiny slip-on shoes. He usually wore a button-hole carnation. Many times I would give him a red carnation button hole which he wore for the show. I haven't mentioned this before, but whenever I heard, or saw, David sing, I cried with emotion. Many of David's fans were the same. When David was on the stage singing, we would sit silent and enraptured, moved with emotion at his beautiful voice so full of sincerity, with the sound of a quiet sob now and again, and at the end we applauded him, but we never screamed.'

The summer season went by very quickly and David and his family were kept busy during the time he was not on the stage. David and the King Brothers were in a team of show business stars who took part in a comic cricket match at Southsea in aid of the Police Widows and Orphans Fund. The match against a select police eleven eventually ended in a draw. Two of his other off-stage duties were to give out the prizes in a children's angling tournament and to be the chief judge in a Miss Gosport beauty competition. There could be little doubt that, despite his affection for children, the latter would have given him the most pleasure. In the Fifties, summer shows were not performed on Sundays, but it did not mean a day off. David dashed North to appear at the Blackpool Opera House on the last two Sundays of August and then appeared in Manchester on the first two Sundays of September. There was also fêtes and other events to open and appear at, usually with Shiela and the children. Mrs. Kelly of Gosport, whose husband served with David in the Royal Navy, remembers 'David appearing at the King's Theatre, Southsea, in the summer of 1957. During that week he attended a garden fête at the Portsmouth Royal Naval Barracks, with his wife and little boy, where I was introduced to him. I remember what an unassuming, friendly person he seemed, unaffected by fame. I was a competition winner that afternoon and he was expected to present prizes, but unfortunately had to leave early in time for an evening performance, otherwise I might have got a kiss as well as a handshake.' I think she could have bet her life on that.

The summer season at Southsea was followed by a return to the North with an engagement at the Winter Gardens, Mŏrecambe, and a short season in Liverpool at the Empire. Shiela and the children had returned to Hull during these shorter engagements, and David continued to stay with friends whenever possible, instead of the more usual and impersonal hotels and guest-houses. He built up a large selection of friends throughout the country by doing this, both male and female, and the majority of these are still very supportive, even many years after his death, through their membership of the two, still active, Societies.

One disappointment in 1957 was that in the *Melody Maker* poll, David dropped to 11th out of 16 in the male singer section. This was down on the previous year and it appeared that the rock and roll artistes were beginning to take a stranglehold on pop music. The good news, at about this time, was that David signed with George and Alfred Black to star in the Blackpool summer season during the following year. This would be David's third summer season out of four at Blackpool.

It seemed that David was acquiring a new and wider fan following at the end of 1957. He still had the loyal original teenagers, although by now most were in their early 20s, but the new 14 and 15-year-olds were ardently following the rock groups – and they did scream! David's new following were a little older than the youngsters who had originally built him up to stardom but they were much more loyal and lasting. This could well have been because his stage show had become a first-class variety act, and in 1957 there was still room for this in show business. A look at the records of a popular sea-side resort like Blackpool in the Fifties show that during the summer season there were no fewer than five variety shows, all with top class entertainers and all playing to packed houses. David was no longer content to offer just a string of recording hits. These were introduced, of course, but only when they fitted into his programme. The adulation of the previous years had been replaced by good honest solid applause as was evident when the *Light Up The Town* show was

taken to Manchester. His years of hard work on the stages of theatres and clubs in the early Fifties were now standing him in good stead.

The year ended with a return to pantomime for David, this time in the star role of Robinson Crusoe at the London Palladium, for the Christmas and New Year season. The veteran comedian Arthur Askey and the up and coming Tommy Cooper were also in the show. Even this booking was not without its problems, as Val

In Robinson Crusoe, *1957*

75

Parnell had decided to break with tradition and cast David as the principal boy instead of the more usual glamorous female. Generally the more popular press liked the idea, but the critic of one prominent Sunday newspaper wrote: '*Robinson Crusoe* was the dullest and dreariest charade I've seen for a long time.' But, whatever the critics thought, the public loved it. Box office receipts and attendance figures showed the pantomime a record breaker, from the time of its opening in December to the final curtain in the following April.

Things were changing for David by the end of 1957. He was beginning to be forced, by the new priorities in show business, to alter his role as strictly a pop singer to that of an all-round entertainer, and in some ways he was far happier playing that part. The next big question was: what changes would 1958 bring?

Chapter Twelve

Cry My Heart **(1958)**

The pantomime *Robinson Crusoe* was so successful, after all, that it was extended until April, after reaching its hundredth performance. This must have been a blow to the traditionalists who had provided so much criticism at the end of the previous year.

The *London Evening News* critic gave an excellent report with the headlines, 'This *Crusoe* is Just Fabulous'. The review went on to say: 'We have been seeing pantomimes for a good many years now and it is hard to recall one to equal this year's fabulous show, *Robinson Crusoe* at the Palladium.

'What Val Parnell and his producer, Robert Nesbitt must have spent on this Daniel Defoe story! If it is a penny under £45,000 we shall be surprised.

'In many ways it is a most unusual pantomime. Men predominate. In fact, apart from the attractive showgirls, the lasses hardly get a look in at all.

'But as Arthur Askey is the Dame there are compensations in plenty. The little man is very, very funny. In a magnificently produced underwater scene, he emerges from a huge pearl to pirouette round the sea-bed to the music of *Swan Lake*. And he has an amusing song, *Hull, Hull Captivating, Fascinating Hull* (as you *Robinson Crusoe* enthusiasts will remember, it was from the Yorkshire seaport that our hero set out).

'We roared with delight at the entrance of Tommy Cooper, crying, "Free, free after 2,000 years in a bottle" and "I've got pins and needles all down my legs". He battles his way through a haze of smoke. The crazy magician is an admirable foil for Arthur Askey.

Biggest surprise comes from David Whitfield in the name part. He has never spoken lines on the stage before. Here he gives a performance of charm and sympathy and sings better than the majority of Robinson Crusoes we have heard.'

The newspaper critic was obviously very pleased with the production, but what about David's fans, more used to him in a dinner jacket on the stage of a variety theatre than in a pantomime?

A fan who had travelled up from Portsmouth specially to see the show looks back 35 years and says: 'The show was wonderful, very colourful, lovely music, it starred Tommy Cooper and Arthur Askey as well as David, so it was very funny. This was the first time David had appeared in a show in which he acted and sang. He was very good, and sang beautifully as ever. He was also very funny in parts. I enjoyed it, but I had to admit to him in a letter that I preferred him in a variety show when he appeared at the end in a dress suit and sang alone. Also it was a pantomime, and I'm not too keen on those anyway. But it was still wonderful to see him again and top of the bill at the Palladium.'

She goes on to say that she went with her friend to the Number One dressing room at the Palladium where David gave them a penny each as a souvenir (one of the pantomime props) and a piece of the material from the costume he wore in the show.

A re-occurrence of David's old throat problems had him preparing to go into the London Clinic at the beginning of February, but, due to the extension of the pantomime's season, he had to postpone the operation until April. Shiela travelled to London to be with him, and afterwards he returned to Hull for a week's recuperation. In an interview with Radio Humberside just before his last visit to Australia, David gave a graphic account of the aftermath of the operation: 'I had to see three throat specialists and they all said: "Get those tonsils out." So I went into the London Clinic and, I'm not kidding, the tonsils were like a pair of golf balls. Arthur Askey rang after the operation and said, "I suppose you can only eat jelly." He must have been joking, they were feeding me lumps of chicken that I had to swallow whole to keep the glottis open.'

It is said, but not confirmed, that David was so proud of the size of the tonsils that he kept them pickled in a jar on his dressing-room table ready to impress any visitors.

The big Whitfield record hit of 1958 was the song, *Cry My Heart,* where David renewed his acquaintance with Mantovani and his Orchestra, a usually infallible combination as far as hit records were concerned. The record did not reach the Top Ten but it came into the Hit Parade in mid-February at Number 22 and remained there for three weeks. The record was released to the United States in March, on the London label, and sold a lot of copies without actually getting into the charts. A record reviewer wrote about the record: 'The Whitfield larynx in powerful form combined with strings to wring the last drop of drama from the ballad, *Cry My Heart.* Both *Cry My Heart* and *My One True Love* should satisfy the most discerning Whitfield fans.'

David made three television appearances in May, a comparative rarity, for the 'box' was still his least favourite method of performance.

He started by being one of the guests in ATV's *Jack Jackson Show*. It was not long after his throat operation, and he had to mime his records because his voice was not quite back to normal. Later in the same month he appeared among the many stars who were invited to celebrate with a big party the hundredth edition of ARTV's *Cool For Cats*. During the evening, the thousandth disc to be played since the series started in the previous summer was heard. It was Anne Shelton's *The Girl He Left Behind*.

Following this, on Saturday 24 May David was seen throughout the ITV network on the *Dave King Show*. These appearances in May were followed by a part in ATV's *Saturday Spectacular*, where he appeared alongside Dickie Valentine in late November. 1958 could be considered as his best year ever for television appearances in the United Kingdom.

The second record release of 1958 was David's recording of *On The Street Where You Live* from the hit show *My Fair Lady*. It was David's biggest hit for nearly two years and reached Number 16 in May, staying in the Top Twenty for 14 weeks. Vic Damone's version appeared at the same time and went to Number One; the Americans were hitting back! Although he did not know it at the time, this was to be his last record anywhere near the top of the Hit Parade. He was to have two more in the charts during the next two years but neither was to remain there for long, only a week in both cases. One of these, his final record release in 1958, *The Right to Love,* entered the Hit Parade at Number 30 in August and then dropped out in just one week. It had all the old Whitfield ingredients for success, good tune and lyrics and an excellent backing, but time, and the record buying public, had marched on, and it was really his old fans who bought enough copies to enable the song to reach its Hit Parade position. He really needed new fans, but the youngsters had gone off in an entirely different musical direction, the way of rock and roll. Among the new breed of singers was Elvis Presley, and not even the top American stars could live with him.

At the end of June David started a long summer season at the Opera House, Blackpool. He topped the bill yet again, and, although his recording success was beginning to wane, he was well able to hold his top billing on the theatre circuit. During the time at Blackpool David was interviewed by *Melody Maker* reporter Jerry Dawson and the subject of his apparent shift away from pop music came up.

'What, me give up singing pop? Not on your life,' said David. His emphatic denial was prompted by the reporter's suggestion that he appeared to be leaning towards the more conventional ballad, and it was David's choice of numbers in his solo spot which had caused the question to be asked. His act consisted of seven songs, and three of them, *Tell Me Tonight, The Song of the Vagabonds,* and *Throw Open Wide Your Window, Dear,* in which he danced a quick waltz with a ballerina in true musical comedy style, would hardly have appealed to the pop-loving teen-ager. Incidentally, waltzing with members of the audience was to get him into trouble in later years.

'But they do,' insisted David. 'I get as much applause for these songs as I do for any of the Hit Parade numbers. I've always liked this type of song and always included them in my act. In fact, I first sang *The Song of the Vagabonds* more than four years ago. 'Ever since I first started singing it has been my ambition to satisfy everybody – I know that's impossible – but you can't blame me for trying. It gives me something to strive for – a sort of self-discipline that keeps me on my toes for my own sake. Before I came to Blackpool, I recorded twelve tracks to be issued as an L.P. in September. Most of them are what you would call "straight" ballads. I'm keeping my fingers crossed for this one.'

That gave Jerry Dawson his opening: 'Surely, that points in the direction I'm suggesting, away from the pop field.'

'Not in the least, it's just that nobody in show business can afford to stand still. This different field is a challenge and a chance to prove to myself that I can do it. It stops me from getting stale.'

As he talked, David was dressing for his role in the next part of the show in a robust windjammer song, *The Rudder and the Rock*, bell-bottom trousers, striped top, blue jacket and 18th-century black boater hat.

'And you don't mind getting dressed up?' he was asked.

'Not so long as it fits the part.' he replied. 'At first I was a little dubious about playing an acting part in pantomime, but I thoroughly enjoyed last Christmas in *Robinson Crusoe*. But I will still sing pops just as long as the public shows that it wants them by buying my records. It was the pop-loving teen-ager who made my career possible. I wouldn't want to lose their support.'

Unfortunately, it seemed at this point in his career he already had. The record buying youngsters can be very fickle and a new generation had arrived to follow the pop groups. Subsequently, even David was reported as saying, 'The screams are no longer there', so even he was beginning to see the end of his hit record career. His theatre and stage career seemed assured, however, judging by the audience's reaction on the first night of the Blackpool summer show.

The year ended with a six-week stint at the Coventry Theatre in a performance called *The Birthday Show* during October and November, followed by a return to the role of Robinson Crusoe at the Birmingham Hippodrome for the Christmas season.

The biggest snag with pantomime roles was that it kept David away from his family for most of the Christmas and New Year holiday. If he did manage to get away, the children were in bed when he arrived home and he had to leave early the next morning. This partly led to another sour note in his success story, as rumours began to circulate about Shiela and David's domestic life. As Shiela later remarked: 'In the beginning they used to hurt, and particularly they used to hurt me. But then, as the years go on, you learn to accept them. At first I used to take them personally, but then we learnt to laugh them off.'

The most hurtful thing for them was that a lot of the rumours about their marriage came from their home town of Hull. David was always one for the ladies and his reputation, for good or bad, went with him. Like all marriages they had gone through good and bad patches and, because of his frequent absences, the bad sometimes tended to be exaggerated. The couple had tried to set a pattern from the beginning of David's professional career where they tried to spend two weeks together before Shiela returned home to the children. During the summer seasons in the sea-side towns they rented a house nearby to keep the family together and Shiela accompanied David on many of his tours abroad in the Fifties and early Sixties. Shiela, being an only child, tended to be much more of a family person and she endeavoured, and to a certain degree succeeded, to make David the same.

Chapter Thirteen

Willingly (1959)

The year started with the continuation of a pantomime performance, which was to be the pattern for David's post-Christmas routine for the next few years. He got his usual good pantomime review: 'The Birmingham Hippodrome production of *Robinson Crusoe* comes direct from the London Palladium in everything except its cast. Bereft of Arthur Askey and Tommy Cooper, it still retains David Whitfield, who strides through it like a veteran. What it lacks in comedy it makes up for in spectacle and song.'

When the pantomime ended, a tour of the North of England began with a week at Huddersfield, followed by appearances at Manchester, Glasgow, Newcastle and Liverpool. The best news of all for David was when, at the beginning of 1959, his international horizons looked as though they were about to be extended, when the Lew and Leslie Grade organisation began negotiations for a concert trip to South Africa. This was due to take place before the start of the summer season at Bournemouth.

New records were still being released, including one called *Willingly* which came out at the same time as an identical record from the singer Johnny Desmond. David's version did not make it into the Hit Parade, but, then, neither did that of Johnny Desmond. The reverse side of David's record was the signature tune from *William Tell*, which had been issued following a demand from avid watchers of the television series starring William Conrad. Surprisingly, that recording did not make any kind of impact on the pop world either.

In April his patience finally ended with the recording company he had been with since the beginning of his professional career, and the following report was printed in a show business magazine: 'Whitfield hits Decca – They won't plug my discs! Gold disc star, David Whitfield, rebelled against Decca's "plug" methods. "They just won't plug my records," he sounded off. David is the second top disc star to clash with Decca in the last six months. In November of last year (1958), Dickie

82

Valentine complained about what he called the almost non-existent exploitation at Decca and the non-release of his records. Currently in Glasgow on a variety tour, Whitfield is to see Decca chief, E.R. Lewis, when he returns to London next month. "I want to know why I'm being treated like this," he said. "There is a big advance order for every one of my records – something like 60,000. Then the sales stick at something like 80,000 to 100,000. It isn't bad I suppose, but sales could be much bigger with the right exploitation."

'Whitfield said he was constantly fighting Decca over which should be the plug side of his discs.

' "One of my recent records, *Cry My Heart* and *My One True Love*, is an example of my grouse," he complained. "Decca decided that *Cry My Heart* was to be the plug side despite the fact that I got lots more reaction to the other side. I couldn't persuade them to work on it. In my opinion, this could have been very big. I still have two years to go with Decca, but, before I re-sign, I shall want to know, in writing, just what exploitation I'm going to get. It's more than a year now since I was in the Hit Parade and I don't think it's because my records aren't good enough. It's simply because they are not being plugged. Decca say I have nothing to worry about. I hope Mr. Lewis can convince me!" ' Obviously, he did not, because 1959 was the first year since 1953 that a David Whitfield record was not in the charts.

A long-playing record, *Hail Variety*, featuring David and many other stars, was produced for the Variety Club of Great Britain by Oriole records and George Elrick, so, as well as David's charity work continuing, he kept to the forefront of the public eye.

It was also apparent that his records were still being played on juke-boxes up and down the country, from a clip in a Kentish newspaper in April: 'Court Hear Whitfield on Juke-box – The strains of David Whitfield's recording of *On the Street Where You Live* echoed around Chatham Court today from a juke-box carried into the building and controlled by a solicitor.' It appeared that the case was concerned with the licensing of music and dancing licences in cafés in the Medway towns. Licences had been refused because the police thought that juke-boxes attracted 'undesirables' to the cafés. The solicitor must have thought that David's tenor voice and ballad type songs would swing the case the way of the café owner. All good free publicity for David.

A few television appearances were made in 1959 as David appeared with the American singing star, Joan Deiner, star of the Broadway and London show, *Kismet*, in the television programme, *Saturday Night at the London Palladium*. David still clung on to his star billing as he agreed to share it, on this occasion, with Joan. Later in the year, in June, he appeared twice more, on *Saturday Spectacular* and Jack Parnell's *Disc Break*.

He continued with the hectic variety touring schedule with visits to Southampton, Huddersfield, Newcastle and Manchester in March, followed by Glasgow, Huddersfield, Liverpool and Belfast in the following month. He still put his fans first, and even now they remember him for the occasional personal kindness not always shown by top performers. A man still living in the area remembers cycling from Portsmouth to Southampton to see David in his act at the Gaumont Theatre: 'I must have been about 12 at the time. I'd always liked David Whitfield and when I heard he was appearing in Southampton I decided to cycle there to see him. After the show I went round to the stage door to see if I could get his autograph. A rather forbidding miserable-looking doorman told me that David wasn't signing any autographs that day and to clear off. I explained that I'd ridden specially from Portsmouth and would he go and ask the singer. After about five minutes, the doorman came back accompanied by David who took me back to his dressing-room, gave me a cup of tea and signed my book. We must have been chatting for about half an hour before I left and headed back home. I've never forgotten his kindness.'

The visit to Manchester was not quite such a happy occasion, as someone stole David's gold watch from the dressing room while he was on stage at the Palace Theatre. The watch had great sentimental value because it had been a Christmas present from Shiela in 1955 and was engraved on the back. It was obviously taken by a thief and not a souvenir hunter because two pound notes went missing at the same time.

A snippet in *The Star* at the beginning of May shows that the Whitfields were preparing to take their usual holiday before David started his summer show, but this time there was a slight hitch: 'The French Riviera for father, Margate for mother and the children. Sounds a bit one-sided but that's the way it has to be for David Whitfield and his family.

'David wanted to take his wife Shiela to Nice for a fortnight's holiday. But Shiela is expecting her third child in three months time and her doctor said she couldn't go.

'So David flew off to the Riviera today for a week on his own. When he comes back, he'll take Shiela and their two children to Margate.'

Summer seasons, like winter pantomimes, were becoming a regular annual feature in David's itinerary. It suited him and the family because it cut down on a lot of the travelling, although he still did the occasional Sunday concert, four in Blackpool during the summer months, but also the family could be with him, even if it was in rented accommodation.

The 1959 summer season was at the Pavilion, Bournemouth, in *The Big Show of 1959*. It started on 2 July and ran for ten weeks, giving his numerous southern fans a chance to see more of him. One of these fans writes from Fareham: 'My home town is Bournemouth, where David had a summer season, that was a bonus for us, no travelling all summer. We went to every show; some people thought we were crazy and I suppose some of the things we got up to were, but they are great memories to look back on. It was just so sad to lose a great friend.'

The Whitfield family was added to in the summer with the birth of a daughter, Amanda Jane, on 1 August. The birth was reasonably uncomplicated, but just a few weeks before, Shiela had been driving her blue Ford Consul saloon with seven-year-old beside her. She swerved to miss a dog and the car veered off the road and crashed into a tree. The front of the car was badly damaged but, fortunately, Shiela and Lance escaped with a few minor cuts and bruises. The unborn baby was also checked and luckily found to be trouble-free.

Throughout his life David was always pleased to see his friends from the Navy. He genuinely liked to talk about old times and the meetings usually developed into a monumental 'booze-up'. One of them, who had served with him on the *Black Swan* and accompanied him ashore in Shanghai, was still in the service in 1959. He made contact with David during his season at Bournemouth: 'The last occasion I saw David was in 1959 when he was starring at the Bournemouth Pavilion. As a newly

At the christening of Amanda Jane, September, 1959   *(Photograph by the late Donald I. Innes. Innes Studio, Hessle)*

commissioned officer, I had recently been appointed to *H.M.S. Trafalgar*. The ship was paying a courtesy visit to Bournemouth and part of the entertainment laid on by the Mayor and Council for the Wardroom was a cocktail party and seats for the theatre. Of course, at the end of the show we were all ushered back stage to meet the cast. Dave, of course, recognised me at once, but, as he was in great demand, said we should have a private get-together and it was arranged for the following evening. I went round between shows and we had a good natter catching up on things. While he was on the stage, I was well looked after by the Tiller Girls. After the show we went out to a Chinese restaurant, a bit of a novelty because they were few and far between in England in those days. After supper he insisted on seeing me back to the jetty to catch the boat.

'Well, if you could have seen the looks on the faces of the other members of the ship's company waiting for the boat. Up rolled a big car, out stepped David Whitfield and a couple of gorgeous Tiller Girls and the newly arrived T.A.S. officer. For me, truly a great send-off and again an evening to be remembered, thanks to Dave. But that was him all over, doing something out of the ordinary; an English dinner in Shanghai, a Chinese meal in Bournemouth.'

David's throat problems made a re-appearance while he was in the Bournemouth show. He had to enter the London Clinic at the beginning of August with a throat infection which was to keep him out of action for four days. Dickie Valentine stepped in for David while he was away. Even this short break did not solve the problem and by the end of the month he was back in the clinic again. This time he was ordered to rest for two days, complete rest without even the telephone, just peace and quiet. Perhaps the Tiller Girls had all been too much for him.

By the beginning of September he seemed to have made a complete recovery and was ready to return to his native town, Hull, for a week's engagement at the Regal. It was the first time for over two years that he had appeared professionally in his home town, and, as many of the criticisms and rumours about his marriage and general behaviour had originated from there, he must have approached the engagement with some trepidation. It turned out that his apprehension was unfounded because he played to packed audiences for the whole week.

Another record was released at this time with high hopes of an entry into the Top Twenty and a good review from the critics: 'Three months have passed since David's last single was issued, so this disc provides a powerful "welcome back" for him. His admirers and the admirers of British song-smith Billy Reid should not miss the record, *Oh Tree*. It will appeal to all ballad lovers.' If it did, it was not indicated by record sales. Perhaps the older record-buying public were now watching television much more than listening to records?

The variety round continued in October and November with

appearances at Hanley, Finsbury Park, in London, Leicester, Leeds and Manchester. The year ended with the inevitable pantomime appearance, this time a change of character and a change in surroundings. David appeared in *Humpty Dumpty on Ice* at the Brighton Palladium, for a minimum of four weeks, according to the pre-season hand-outs. Later comments by a theatre critic and a fan give a good indication of the success of the show. The critic wrote: 'Appearing on 850 square-feet of ice, David Whitfield effectively used every inch of it in *Humpty Dumpty* at Brighton's Palladium. Strolling casually around with a button-hole mike and 150 feet of cable, David is a decided hit and should attract big business.'

On the same subject, and about the same show, Mrs W. wrote from Havant: 'On one occasion, David was the singing star in *Humpty Dumpty on Ice* at the Palladium, Brighton. My husband, son and I went to the New Year's Eve performance. After the show David sang some of his hit songs. As we listened, the time for catching the train back home got nearer, but I just could not leave. My husband and son left the theatre to catch the train, and with great reluctance I eventually followed, running all the way to the station, avoiding the many New Year revellers. Now an O.A.P., I still play my David Whitfield records. He will always be the greatest singing star for me.' A fitting note to end the Fifties, a decade when David Whitfield had more records in the charts than any other Englishman and, although his record sales were now falling away, still held star billing on the variety circuit. A decade which had began with his early variety appearances with Hughie Green, where he had soared to international stardom in the mid-Fifties and now at the end was fighting hard to keep his top billing against the relentless march of rock and roll.

Great social changes in popular music and entertainment had taken place during this period. In the early Fifties dancing had taken place to the big bands with their resident singers. The cinema and variety theatre were big business with long queues of eager customers at the weekends and during holiday time. These were gradually replaced by television viewing and performances by groups of skifflers and rock and rollers. A good indication of the influence of television in entertainment is shown by the fact that in 1950 only two of the 40 pages of the *Radio Times* were devoted to television programmes. By 1959 there were twelve television pages out of 48. The tendency was away from cinema and live theatre and David Whitfield must have realised that his great star times had been and gone. He was forced to make the big decision on which direction to take to secure for himself a comfortable future in show business.

Chapter Fourteen

Angela Mia (1960)

The year 1960 not only introduced a new decade; it also showed a change in David's fortunes and show business format. The Sixties were to be the pop period of the Beatles, Rolling Stones, Hollies, Manfred Mann and Cliff Richard, all many miles away from David Whitfield's ballad style of singing.

It was ten years since he had left the Navy and a lot had happened. He had been up to the heights of stardom and as far as records were concerned was on his way down. It also had to be admitted that, although he was making enough money with variety, television and radio appearances, even here the automatic top billing was beginning to fade. Reg Williams, one of David's oldest friends and confidants, a well-known club owner in Hull, remembers David coming to see him about this time on one of his visits to his home town. 'What are you going to do when your voice starts to go and you can't reach some of the notes you need?' asked Reg. Tears came to David's eyes and he went into the middle of the room and belted out a song at the top of his voice.

'What's wrong with that voice?' he asked.

'Nothing,' said Reg. 'But you've got to face up to the fact that sooner or later you won't be able to sing as well as you do now.' Incidentally, Reg Williams always swore that David's voice was much better as a natural voice before he received advice and tuition from voice and elocution 'experts'.

David must have taken note, although it is probable it had been on his mind for a couple of years, because one of the things he did in 1960 was to go over to light operetta and musical shows. Whether this was a wise move or not only show business history can judge, but he was certainly keeping up to his own maxim of changing to suit the times. There was no way he could change to the rock and roll sphere of show business so logically, the 'musical' was the right way to go. Nevertheless, this area of music was pretty well covered by the likes of John Hanson and Ted Hockridge and there were plenty of ballad singers on both sides of the

Atlantic who survived the rock onslaught and went on to greater things.

Before the change to musicals, the other big event of 1960 was David's tour of Australia. He had been very disappointed when the proposed South African visit of the previous year did not materialise and the Australian tour did a lot to raise his spirits, although it meant leaving his family again, this time for nearly half a year. Before going off to the other side of the world he continued with his charity work by autographing LPs, which were then auctioned at a theatrical ball in aid of show business charities at the Glasgow City Chambers on 11 February.

It seems that he had also changed his original ideas about appearing on television because he pre-recorded four shows for ATV before leaving for Australia. The 35-minute programmes, with other guest stars and the orchestra directed by David's own musical director, Paul Conrad, were to be screened during the singer's absence. He also featured in a farewell ATV *Saturday Spectacular* at the end of February, so more television appearances seemed also to be a very important part of his new image.

With all his pre-tour commitments completed, David flew off to the country where ultimately he was to plan to settle, and also prematurely meet his death. The *Hull Daily Mail* reported: 'Hull-born singer, David Whitfield, leaves his Kirkella home tomorrow en route to Australia, where he'll be appearing in variety for six months. Seeing him off from London Airport will be his wife Shiela and their three children, Lance(7), Shane(2) and 8-month-old Amanda Jane. Mrs Whitfield is flying out to join her husband in Sydney at the beginning of May. He opens his tour in Melbourne.' (In fact, Shiela left England to join David in Australia on 27 May.)

A newsletter to members of the fan club, dated March 1960, gives a good impression of Shiela's feelings as David, with his musical director, Paul Conrad, and manager, Peter Lavoie, flew off to Australia. He had been abroad before but not for the length of time of this tour. It must have been a bit like one of his old naval commissions, with a lot more luxury. Shiela wrote: 'On Thursday evening, the day before we left Hull, we had a small house party at *Cara Mia*. Close friends and neighbours came along, and also some of our relations. We all had a thoroughly enjoyable time, but all too quickly it was time for them to go, for in our house on Friday morning we had to be up early and off to London.

'So on Friday, Nanny, Lance and Shane travelled down by train from Hull. David and I drove down by car, and then we met Nanny and the children at King's Cross Station and we all travelled to the hotel together. We felt that Amanda Jane was much too young to travel down, so she stayed at home to mind the house for us. After calling into the London office to say cheerio to everybody, David came back to the hotel and spent the rest of the afternoon playing with Lance and Shane. All too quickly time arrived for them to go to bed, and for us to go out for a small farewell party with friends. After an enjoyable time, we finally arrived back at our hotel at midnight. Time by then was going, much too quickly.

'On the Saturday morning we had to be up at 7 a.m., as the car was calling for us before 8.30 a.m. And so we arrived at the airport just after nine, where they took us straight through to the private lounge where we had coffee while we were waiting.

'You can imagine, there was quite a crowd at the airport to say cheerio. Paul's wife and daughter had come along to wave him on his way. Peter's wife, also some friends of his were there to say cheerio to him, and on David's side, Lance, Shane, Nanny and myself.

'Besides this, there were quite a lot of fans ready to wave goodbye to David as well . . . Suddenly it was one mad rush to say cheerio and, before we knew what had happened, David, Paul and Peter had been whisked into a coach to take them to the plane.

'We were led out to a balcony where we could watch the plane take off. Luckily, we were able to see them climb into the plane quite clearly, and then, as the plane started off, it taxied close by to where we were standing, and so we were able to wave goodbye to them properly.'

The journey to Australia in 1960 was not quite the smooth effortless travel of today. They travelled in a giant Comet Four airliner to Singapore, stopping to re-fuel at Athens, Tehran, Karachi, Colombo and Kuala Lumpur. From Singapore they travelled to Jakarta where the new plane developed engine trouble and they were forced to remain there for six hours, eventually taking off for Perth, their first landfall in Australia. Peter Lavoie writing in the April/May edition of the newsletter describes this: 'Our first glimpse of Australia was Perth. This is a really glorious city, but unfortunately we did not have enough time to move from the airport. However, the weather was beautiful, and luncheon was served in the airport restaurant. All too soon we were back on the aircraft again and the final stage of the journey, arriving in Melbourne at 9.30 p.m. on the Monday evening. After a good night's sleep at the Australia Hotel, Melbourne, we were then ready to commence rehearsals for the *New Faces of 1960* production at the Tivoli Theatre.'

David opened his first performance in Australia on Wednesday, 16 March. It is interesting to note some of his fellow artistes in the show; Joe Baker and Jack Douglas, Chris Cross, The Flat Tops, The Butler Brothers, Bill Wareham and Marcia and Betty Costello. Not quite the exalted company of shows in the mid-Fifties but nevertheless a fresh start.

Even while he was away, David was still trying hard to re-enter the pop scene. His latest recordings, *Angela Mia* and *A Tear, a Kiss, a Smile*, were reviewed at the time in Britain: 'It will soon be holiday time again, and time for the annual wave of Italian songs. David Whitfield's *Angela Mia* is issued at the right moment and will help from television appearances.

appearances. He could put himself back in the Top Twenty.' He did not. Once again his rival from the States, Vic Damone, took first place, but after all he did have Italian ancestry.

David arrived back at London Airport on Sunday, 25 July, after a very successful tour which was to pave the way for frequent visits to Australia over the next twenty years. Not only did he play to huge appreciative audiences but he also kept up the public relations work, which seemed slightly better than the average artiste's method of just going through the motions, as a letter to the *Hull Daily Mail* indicates: 'A big "Thank You" goes to singer David Whitfield from Hull-born Maurice King and his family, for the most enjoyable 10 minutes of our 10 years in Australia." In a letter from Victoria, Australia, Mr. King, who was well known in Hull boxing and football circles, writes of a backstage meeting with David during the singer's recent Australian tour. "Told on the phone that some people from Hull wanted to see him, in no time at all, David was out to see us," writes Mr King. The singer invited the whole family, including wife, Dorothy and sons Maurice and Richard, into his dressing room, and posed for their camera. 'Please, Mr. Editor, would you thank David through your newspaper for us. The interview he gave us meant more to us than you can put in writing,' ended the letter.

After a short rest, David began rehearsals for the leading role in Tom Arnold and Leslie A. McDonnell's presentation of *Rose Marie* at London's Victoria Palace, which was due to begin on 22 August. He starred with two comparatively new female singers, Stephanie Voss and Maggie Fitzgibbon. The show was not generally as successful as his pantomime roles, as the article by critic, Norman Heath, shows, although he was not quite so hard on David: *'Rose Marie*, smash hit of the Twenties and now suffering yet another revival at London's Victoria Palace, should have been kept dead and buried. The ancient time-worn plot, seen through the 1960 eyes, the production and performance does not help, or the bad casting. Poor David Whitfield, he tries hard and sings well despite the pit orchestra, but this production just was not his cup of tea. Let's hope he gets another chance in a part better suited to his talents. He's earned it after this.'

It's interesting to compare this review with the record sleeve issued by Decca, in conjunction with the show, *Extracts from Rose Marie,* where David sang with Jan Waters: 'The production of *Rose Marie* which was launched at London's Victoria Palace, Autumn 1960, with David Whitfield in a starring role, is part of a bold experiment designed to pull back into some of the nation's most important variety theatres the thousands of "regulars" who were driven away from their favourite seats in the stalls by the prolonged attacks of the untalented invaders who ushered in the era of Rock.

'A seemingly endless parade of youthful rockers draped themselves about the powerful microphones and proudly displayed the shiny, scarcely-fingered guitars which hung about their chests, to eager audiences of bewitched worshippers.

'Truly, the theatres were well filled by the teenagers, but this type of entertainment brought but a short box office peak. Now that skiffle has scuttled back into its rightful crevice somewhere between the adjacent portals of New Orleans jazz and Negro folk song and the merchants of rock have modified their merchandise to make it less jarring upon the nerves, far-seeing impresarios have seen the necessity of attracting afresh their old customers and at the same time retaining the enthusiastic support of the younger newcomers.

'David Whitfield in *Rose Marie* has proved to be one of the successful answers to their problem. The musical, originally seen at Drury Lane in 1925, was given something of a theatrical face-lift to make it suitable for the streamlined production tactics of the Sixties.'

In later years some of these comments, and they apparently echoed the official Decca line, seem rather misplaced. The 'youthful' rockers were going to be around, in one form or another, for a very long time. Also, Decca, along with most of the record companies, had elected to jump on the same rock and roll band-waggon which sold millions of records, and it was hardly likely that they would bite the hand that fed them. It rather seemed they were hedging their bets in both directions after David and Dickie Valentine's criticisms about plugging their records in previous years.

Rose Marie actually played at the Victoria Palace for 17 weeks and then the whole production moved to Scotland for a Christmas season at Edinburgh and a four-weeks' stay in Glasgow which took them into the New Year. David's usual pantomime role was thus replaced by a musical show. This gave the family the opportunity to return to Hull for Christmas and the New Year as, while David was appearing in London, they had been renting a house in Cheam, Surrey – what the *Hull Daily Mail* laughingly called *Hancock-land.*

But what did his fans think of the show and David's changed role? One of the most devoted says: 'In 1960 David was at the Victoria Palace in *Rose Marie*. I managed to go every week on a Wednesday to see him. I saw the show nearly every week, he was wonderful in it. I wish I could have seen him in more of these sort of shows. He was wonderful in *Rose Marie*. To my great regret I never saw him in *The Desert Song*. It didn't come to the South. I did save up every penny I could to spend a few days in Coventry with another fan when David was there, but, alas, the very week we were there, David was away, sick with tonsillitis.'

1960 had been quite a hectic year, mostly taken up with the tour of Australia and the show, *Rose Marie,* but this was by no means all of his engagements. Apart from the television appearances while he was away, he continued the Sunday concert tours in the late summer and autumn with one-day appearances at Blackpool, Bridlington, Morecambe, Leicester, Doncaster, Peterborough and Hull. He appeared at one of his favourite venues, Blackpool, where he was always assured of a warm welcome, three times during August and September.

A surprise hit record occurred at the end of the year with a re-issue of one of his earliest hits, *I Believe*, that had brought him fame seven years before. This time it only crept into the Hit Parade for one week in November. It did not herald an upsurge in his record sales. In fact, it was the last time that David appeared in the Hit Parade; his hit record career had lasted exactly seven years.

Chapter Fifteen

Farewell to Decca (1961-64)

In 1961 David finally parted company with the Decca recording company after eight years and 28 records in the Hit Parade. Some of this number were re-entries but, even so, that is a lot of record sales. During his recording career with Decca, David, now 35, had recorded many hits, including *Cara Mia* and *I Believe*, but it had been some time since he had a record in the Top Ten, four years to be precise.

He signed a three-year contract with HMV, whose top British artistes included Ronnie Hilton and Bert Weedon. There is little doubt that Decca had the best years out of David, and made thousands of pounds out of his style of singing. David's manager, Peter Lavoie, diplomatically explained the move by saying: 'After eight years with Decca, it was felt that it would be a good thing to have a change.'

One of the last recordings he made with Decca was released in April. It was a long-player, backed by Paul Conrad and his Orchestra, and contained a lot of the old musical ballads written by such composers as Rodgers, Hammerstein and Jerome Kern. It was an easy listening record that had reasonable sales but nowhere near enough to indicate some sort of comeback in the pop world. It seemed that David had given up that area of show business for good.

The change certainly did not show any immediate effect because 1961 was a relatively quiet year. After the Christmas and New Year engagements in Scotland, the show, *Rose Marie*, with David, headed south and he was actually appearing at the Grand Theatre, Wolverhampton, when he changed record companies.

He continued to perform at Sunday concerts, appearing at Bradford, Gloucester and Portsmouth during the Spring of 1961, while *Rose Marie* did the rounds of the country. One of David's most ardent fans remembers him appearing at the Guildhall at Portsmouth on 21 May of that year: 'I didn't see David back-stage at the Guildhall, but I had a seat in the front row, and David saw me. He knew I was going through a worrying time, and he sang *You'll Never Walk Alone* all the way through just for me. I know, because his eyes looked straight at mine as he sang, and he sang so sincerely and emotionally . . .'

Not everything went smoothly with the fans, however. On a visit to Newcastle, some autograph-hunting fans, mostly girls, waiting outside the stage door, were soaked when dirty water was poured on them from an upstairs window. David is reported to have said at the time: 'I think it was a childish trick. If I find out who it was, I will deal with them.'

David also seemed to be jinxed as far as injuries were concerned during this year. He had always considered himself pretty fit, as with such an onerous touring and one-day appearance schedule, he could not really be anything else. A newspaper report of the time stated: 'Injury jinx hits David Whitfield! An injury hoodoo hovers over singer David Whitfield. In Dover he broke a foot. In Birmingham he gashed his head. In Finsbury Park he had a hand injury. In a Palladium pantomime he hurt a leg... And last weekend at Liverpool's Empire David slipped and broke two bones in his hand. Said David: "I'll only postpone a concert when my voice, not my hand, is broken. Show business seems a worse occupation for injuries than soccer." '

There was little doubt at this time that David was drinking more than usual. Nagging doubts about his ability to sing as well as ever and worries about his apparent inability to regain his record chart status all combined to make him more insecure than ever before in his life. David, normally a very confident man – 'the most confident man I ever met', according to his later musical director, Bert Gaunt – was going through a worrying time, and the normal few pints of beer and a game of darts in a nearby pub, before a show had changed to a bottle of vodka in his dressing room. There is a well-known story in showbiz circles that most tenors have a glass of whisky before a performance in order to 'lubricate the throat'. It is also true in some cases that the glass becomes two and then three and so on. David had not got to the stage of over-drinking that was to occur later in his career, but the first signs were there. It seems more than a coincidence that, after years of accident-free performances, all these minor injuries began now.

Only two appearances were made on television and radio in 1961, an act in ITV's *Sunday Night at the London Palladium* in early March, and one on radio's *Blackpool Night* during the summer season at Blackpool.

David was back at Blackpool during the summer, still with the touring, *Rose Marie*. Despite the early criticism, the show was to play for over a year, going on to Brighton and Bristol for two-week periods in the Autumn. The show finally finished at Bristol, and David must have been glad of a change after doing the same show for so long.

He returned to pantomime over the Christmas period 1961-2 with an appearance in *Sleeping Beauty* at the Grand Theatre, Leeds. Further down the bill from David were the up-and-coming comedy pair, Eric Morecambe and Ernie Wise.

Although Leeds was not very far from Hull, the danger of driving in fog and on icy roads meant that he had to stay in Leeds. Shiela had tried to rent a house in the Leeds area for the duration of the pantomime, with no success. An interview in the *Hull Times* with her, ten days before the pantomime opened, gives an indication of some of the problems faced by show business families: 'We've been looking for a house for one or two months and still we haven't found one. Of course, a lot of people, once they know you're theatricals, just turn you down flat. That's because some people in this profession just don't bother to look after the houses or flats they rent and hold riotous parties late at night. We aren't party-goers ourselves and can't give many, because of the three children. But we still can't get a house.'

She went on to mention some of the problems involved in moving the Whitfield family away for a three-month period: 'We have to take virtually everything except the furniture. All our clothes, pots, pans, children's toys, bed linen and, when the baby, Amanda Jane, was younger, the cot, playpen and high chair, as well as the dog basket and the dog.'

During the pantomime rehearsals, David managed to get away for the weekend for another appointment that was always very important to him, the annual party at the Hesslewood Orphanage in Hull. He had promised

At Hesslewood Orphanage, 1961

(Picture courtesy Hull Daily Mail)

to sing and, although the party was for grown-ups, on this occasion he was hoping to raise money for the children's benefit. Both he and Shiela were on the committee of the Orphanage and he was always bringing the establishment's need for funds to the notice of his show business friends and acquaintances, usually to very good effect.

David's publicity machine must have faltered during the folllowing year, 1962. He made many more appearances than in the previous year, but very little was reported, either in newspapers or theatre or music magazines. This was not altogether a bad thing if he had only known what kind of publicity was to come in the next few years.

His main engagement was in the role of the Red Shadow in the *Desert Song*, usually the domain of the tenor John Hanson. David was back on the road again as the show toured from April to November that year, visiting 11 cities for periods of from one to three weeks. The injury jinx struck again during this show, when he not only injured himself but his leading lady as well, as a newspaper clipping at the time reports: 'Whitfield was carrying Miss Page up a flight of stairs at the rear of the stage, at the interval curtain, when he fell with Miss Page in his arms. After a lengthy hold-up, during which apologies were made to the audience, the show carried on with Whitfield's understudy, Howarth Nuttall, who plays one of the supporting roles, taking over as the Red Shadow. Miss Page hurt her right arm in the fall but carried on. David Whitfield limped on to the stage at the final curtain and congratulated his stand-in and sang the *Desert Song* theme song in response to calls from

David as the Red Shadow in Desert Song

97

With Sheffield Shopping Queen, Ann Whittaker, at the opening of the city's Christmas shopping season

the audience. A spokesman for the company said that Whitfield had a badly sprained ankle and was given a pain-killing injection before he went on the stage for the final curtain.'

The rest of his time between the pantomime and *Desert Song* appearances was taken up with the usual Sunday concerts at seaside resorts. He performed ten in all, from the Isle of Man to Margate, during the summer and early autumn months in 1962. During these concerts he apparently fell out with Joan Regan when they were both appearing at Blackpool, and she appeared top of the bill at the end of the second half of the show. The pressure of top billing, or rather, the loss of it, was beginning to show.

Sometimes the old happy-go-lucky David still emerged, as at the time when he was appearing in Sheffield in *The Desert Song*. He was asked to drive in a horse-drawn landau with the Sheffield Shopping Queen, Ann Whittaker, to open the Christmas shopping season. The horse, 'Daisy', involved in the exercise, who pulled a scrap cart normally during the week, decided to stop before she reached the shopping centre and would not budge. David's old horse-driving experience, from many years before in Hull, came to the fore and he took over the reins and persuaded the horse to move on.

At the end of the year he appeared in the pantomime, *Sleeping Beauty*, again with Morecambe and Wise, now moved to the Empire, Liverpool, artistes being the Vernon Girls and The Dallas Boys.

His Sundays were taken up once again with one-day concerts at various sea-side resorts, all in the North. The number of concerts was slightly down on the previous year but this was made up for by the radio show and several celebrity appearances. While he was appearing in Morecambe, he met his old mentor, Hughie Green, again, when he was one of the judges at the 'Miss Great Britain 1963' contest. Judging alongside David were the boss of Moss Empires, Hughie Green, and Jimmy Jewell and Ben Warriss.

David still had a considerable following of fans who had started with him as teen-agers in the early Fifties and faithfully followed him through the rock and roll years. Among these were a real hard core who knew him well enough to be welcomed to his dressing room wherever he appeared. One of their reminiscences makes interesting reading to show the kind of adoration and devotion they felt for him: 'Lots of David's fans would spend their holidays wherever David was appearing during the summer. I could never afford to do this. I could only go on day-trips along the South Coast or to London to see him... I saw David several times during the week he was at the South Parade Pier (Southsea). One evening, back-stage, he asked me if I would like to spend the next day with him. Of course, I said yes, and was so thrilled. Although I saw David many times backstage, this was the only time I saw him away from a theatre. I hardly slept that night, but in the morning I had a slight sore throat. I was horrified, dreading the thought that I might give it to him. I went, anyway, hoping and praying I wouldn't give it to him. I had to wait opposite the Pendragon Hotel where he was staying, by his car, which was a Ford Consul, I think, anyway, it was blue. The number plate was DW100, he always used this number on all his cars. I looked up at the windows of the hotel. I saw David at one of them. He was waving at me. He came down and greeted me with his usual smile and friendly way. He said we must go to the theatre first to sort out the mail. We then had a milk shake in the café on the pier. David asked me if I would like to play golf with him. I said yes, but I had never played golf before. He said never mind, he would teach me, it was only at the miniature golf course by the Canoe Lake. I wasn't much good, but David was very patient with me. I'm afraid I accidentally hit another man's golf ball, and he came over and was very rude and told me off. David was very angry with him and I saw him in a temper for the first time... He said we would go to a pub for lunch. It was a beautiful summer's day and David had the roof down on his car. He switched a tape on in the car, the first time I had ever seen a car radio and tape. It was Christine Campbell singing a song called *My Love For You.* David sang with it as we drove along the sea front and lots of people heard him and looked round. We went to a pub near Portsmouth dockyard, I can't remember the name of it, but it seemed to be on an island with water round, but it can't have been because we drove there. David knew the people who ran the pub. We had a lovely lunch outside by the water and then David had a game of darts. We then drove to Southsea Common and David said he was tired. He lay down on the grass and went to sleep. I didn't want to go to sleep, so I just sat by and watched him. I wanted to savour every moment of this wonderful day...'

1963 ended and 1964 started with another pantomime, *Goldilocks and the Three Bears,* at the Lyceum, Sheffield. It was in this show that David had to throw a baton in the air during the performance. As usual, he went over the top and borrowed a heavy naval mace from the Navy Recruiting Office. According to Bert Gaunt, his musical director, he used to hurl it up as high as he could so that it disappeared up into the lights at the top of the stage. Amazingly enough, he always managed to catch it on the way down!

This was the first pantomime in which David was not top of the bill, another sign that his popularity was beginning to wane. Nevertheless, the show went on until mid-March with 119 performances, and it played to packed audiences. There were no Sunday concerts this year and David had the opportunity, for the second year running, to spend a holiday abroad with his family in early April. This time they visited Holland.

Another services tour followed when he went to Singapore and Malaya from 16 April for three weeks. Later on in the same year, David played to service audiences in South Africa when he visited Cape Town and Johannesburg. It was yet another area of show business, and one that David enjoyed because in a lot of cases it meant he renewed acquaintance with some of his old naval mates. Shiela went with him on this trip so that the after-show naval re-unions did not get out of hand. Unfortunately, it meant that he was out of the public and media eye in the United Kingdom.

He was still in demand for summer shows, his old variety experience making him an instant hit with sea-side holidaymakers. The summer show in 1964, at the Britannia Theatre, Great Yarmouth, was called *All in Favour*. A review from the *Melody Maker* in July said: 'David Whitfield and Eve Boswell may no longer be teen-age idols, but the reception given to them at the first night of Tom Arnold's *All in Favour* at the Brittania Pier proved they are still the tops for a holiday audience.'

David had a change of venue for his pantomime appearance at the end of 1964. He moved back to his native Yorkshire, to the Grand Theatre in Leeds, but appeared in the same show as the previous year, *Goldilocks and the Three Bears*, still presumably throwing the mace.

1964 seemed to be another low point in David's show business career: no television or radio performances, only one concert booking and hardly any kind of national publicity. This was the year the Beatles burst on to the entertainment scene and the pop world in Britain and America was never to be the same again.

Chapter Sixteen

Bad News (1965-66)

After the comparative quiet of the previous year, 1965 heralded a change in routine for David. The pantomime continued until 20 February and then the main change was a return to entertaining in the Northern clubs. Apart from seaside theatres, he was probably happiest in the clubs and felt most at ease with this form of entertainment. This was not too surprising, as his very earliest performances before achieving stardom were in the many clubs in and around his native Hull. The tour of the clubs was followed by a week at the Grand Theatre, Wolverhampton, and Easter at Bridlington. During April and early May, performances in North-eastern theatres and clubs were made. 1965 was also noticeable for a return to the Sunday holiday venue concerts, and, what was more important in the mid-Sixties, a return to television. He appeared in the nationwide television anniversary show of *Saturday Night at the London Palladium* on the ITV network in mid-September. A critic in a national newspaper was not very kind in reviewing the show, writing: 'Among the stars was David Whitfield. Also appearing with David were Joan Regan and Gracie Fields, a convincing argument for beat groups!'

David's summer shows continued with a season at Morecambe's Winter Gardens in a show called *Summer Spectacular*. He was not topping the bill this time, but at least he was welcomed and fully employed for the summer months. The *Melody Maker* review in July was much kinder than that of the Palladium reviewer: 'There are no flies on David Whitfield! No one knows better than he that the days of teenage adulation for his type of singing have gone. And he also knows that there is little point in living in the past, trying to re-create a past image, which is why his contribution to this year's *Summer Spectacular* at the Winter Gardens, Morecambe, contains only one of his past hits, *Cara Mia*. A large chunk of his act is taken up with a little girl and boy from the audience to whom he sings *Daddy's Little Girl* and *Sonny Boy*, strictly for family audiences. And the family audiences loved it.'

David's eldest son, Lance, gives an amusing insight to this part of audience participation: 'Part of Dad's act used to involve getting a little girl up from the audience, sitting her on his knee, and singing *Daddy's Little Girl*. After he'd finished he used to scour the audience for a suitable little boy to sit on his other knee so he could sing *Sonny Boy*. If a nice little chap couldn't be found, the name, "Lance!", would reverberate around the auditorium, at which point some stage-hand would gently push me out of the wings and into the limelight. I would then be scooped up and placed firmly on the knee opposite the little girl. All this instilled in me not so much a feeling of apprehension or alarm but more of just basic fear! I used to love being in the 'wings' and backstage during a show, but just before Dad shouted, "Lance", I used to be through the stage-door and out of that theatre like greased lightning. Upon my return the stage hands used to ask me where I'd been because Dad had wanted me.'

The fact that David had hardly any publicity in the previous few years was unfortunately reversed in 1965, with publicity that he did not really want or need. An incident in a Chesterfield club, just before Christmas, resulted in David deciding to sue a husband for assault. Although he won the case, it really did not do his professional image a lot of good, and whoever advised him to go that far really under-estimated the backlash. Some of his fellow performers felt that he had finally pushed his luck with the ladies too far and that he had got his just deserts.

The local newspaper report read: 'Singer David Whitfield plans to see a solicitor about the black eye he received while serenading a pretty girl in a night-club. "I just can't drop the matter," said the blond singer. "My looks have been quite badly damaged."

'David got his black eye and swollen face at the Carlton Cabaret Club, Chesterfield, where he was topping the bill. He was singing the popular Mary Poppins number, *A Spoonful of Sugar*, in a table to table routine. Leaning across towards a girl at one of the tables, he was grabbed by the hair by a man sitting with her and hit in the face. Stunned and bleeding from a cut below his left eye, David continued the number and went on to finish his act before going to Chesterfield Royal Hospital where five stitches were put in the cut.'

David said afterwards that the routine was a usual part of his act and that he had picked out the same girl to dance with earlier in the evening. He said he had kissed her and then taken her back to a table of about 12 people and that it was a personal part of his act which the girls generally loved and was all part of show business.

The case did go to Derbyshire Quarter Sessions in March of the following year, 1966, and, although David won the case and was awarded damages, the defence, and husband's plea 'that the wife was frightened, upset and embarrassed' did not show him in a very good light. It also seemed that, during the time in the court that he was being questioned, a lot of his natural arrogance seemed to take over, although David probably thought he was being clever. Shiela, interviewed after the trial said: 'I was terribly sorry about the whole thing. I'd been to see my husband's act hundreds of times and he'd kissed young, middle-aged and older women and no one had complained before.' There can also be little doubt that drink played a large part in the incident. As he was top of the bill it was quite easy to spend most of the early evening drinking in the bar, and, very often, David was well under the influence when his turn came to appear.

But the worst was yet to come in 1966, when he was accused of indecent assault by an autograph-hunting 11-year-old girl in Wales. After the aftermath of the court case in Chesterfield had began to die down, and in show business terms any publicity was good within reason, David had settled down to a weekly routine of performances in various clubs in the North and Wales, with the prospect of a summer season in Llandudno. The show was to be called *Gaytime*, a title that was perfectly acceptable in 1966.

Unfortunately, this was one of the summer seasons when Shiela and the children did not accompany him and David was staying with his manager at a bungalow at Glan Conway, reasonably close to the theatre at Llandudno. The case was held at Llanrwst Magistrates Court, Denbighshire, on 10 and 11 October and was reported not only in local newspapers but also in the national press. The prosecuting counsel opened by saying: 'By reason of his talents Whitfield was popular with both young and elderly people. From time to time, young people endeavoured to obtain signed photographs which he was only too willing to give. The girls called at the bungalow to obtain photographs. Two of them were sisters from Colwyn Bay who were staying at Conway. At the bungalow they looked through a window and saw a dark haired man in bed. They went to the kitchen door, which was opened by a man who said he was David Whitfield. He told the girls he could not give them photographs then, because his manager was there, and asked them to call again in the afternoon.

'The girls returned about 3.45 and saw a large car outside. They went again to the kitchen door, and Whitfield agreed to give the girls the photographs they required and went outside to his car. He was wearing a sun suit and short trousers, and sat in the car with one leg outside, while he autographed the photographs. The elder of the two sisters would say that, while in this position, Whitfield indecently exposed himself.

'He then called the girls, one by one, to receive their photographs. All of them then returned to the kitchen. There the question arose of the girls being given some rock. Whitfield went back to the boot of his car where there were some sticks of rock which apparently he was in the habit of giving to children. Whitfield told the girls, with the exception of the older sister, to go back to the bungalow. As this girl was looking down into the boot of the car, Whitfield put his hand down the front of her dress. She pushed him away, and Whitfield told her, "I won't do anything to hurt you".'

The prosecuting counsel went on: 'Back at the bungalow, Whitfield told the girls it was time for them to go, but asked the older sister to stay behind.

'He then asked her if she could come to tea by herself the next day. She replied that she would do so if she could bring her eight-year-old sister with her.'

'Whitfield', said the prosecution, ' asked the girl not to tell anybody about it. Whether this referred to what had taken place, or about returning on the Sunday, might be conjecture.

'Whitfield made the girl give a promise about this several times, and on the way home with her sister and friends the girl started to cry, because she was a Girl Guide and had given this promise.

'The girl's aunt would say that when she returned she was crying and distressed. The girl told her aunt exactly what had happened.

'When seen by the police, Whitfield completely denied the allegations.'

Throughout the hearing, David, who pleaded not guilty to both charges, emphatically denied the charges, describing them as ridiculous. He said that, wearing a sun suit consisting of a vest and shorts, he sat in the back seat of his car with one leg outside while he signed photographs. Because of his unusual position the alleged offence could well have been an unfortunate accident. He went on to say that, while getting three sticks of 'David Whitfield rock' out of the boot of his car, he put his hand on the shoulder of this one girl.

There was another surprise during the second day of the trial. Only one witness was called by the defence, an attractive blonde from Lancashire. She said that she had known David for about seven or eight years and was staying at the bungalow when the children called. She was in the bedroom and heard what transpired. She said the children talked with the singer for about five minutes and then left, with no sign of anything unusual having occurred. Cross-examined by the prosecutor, she said she did not see what had happened, because she was asked to keep out of sight for obvious reasons. The defence counsel followed by saying that it was not often that an advocate was able to place before a court evidence such as that given by the defence witness. He went on: 'Is it likely that this man would choose to behave indecently with little girls when his girl friend is a few yards away to hear any outcry or complaint? You see that she is not an unattractive young lady. So is it likely that he would indulge himself with these children?

'We have a man of 40 who is married and has a wife and three children. He and Miss W. were staying together in this bungalow. That might not be a very creditable thing to do, but this is not a court of morals.'

He added that if anything untoward had happened the magistrates might well think that the witness would have heard something.

The police sergeant, during cross examination, agreed that David was a man of good character, married with three children, including a daughter of seven.

After the five-hour hearing, David was fined the maximum of £25 and ordered to pay £25 costs on a charge of indecent exposure to an eleven-year-old girl. He was acquitted on the other charge of indecently assaulting the same girl by putting his hand down the front of her dress.

'At the end of the case, David was driven away from the court, while women shoppers and schoolgirls surged around the car smiling and waving,' according to a newspaper report. Obviously, the case had not lost him all his fans but it did have a considerable effect on his popularity nationwide at the time.

Readers can make up their own minds about the outcome of the case. Once again drink seemed to take an active part in the incident. Apparently David spent most afternoons during the summer show drinking heavily. It was also a well-known fact that David was too lax in allowing young female fans into his dressing room. Two of his confidants and life-long friends, one of them the television compère, Hughie Green, said that they had warned him on several occasions about the dangers of having teen-age girls hanging about his dressing rooms. David, with his devil-may-care attitude to life, never seemed to take any notice and could be said to take his maxim of 'looking after his fans' too literally.

Several years after the case David gave a written statement about the affair to a friend who was compiling a volume on the Whitfield career. He wrote that he was appearing at the Variety and Sporting Club, Spennymoor, at the time of the hearing: 'Bert Gaunt, my personal pianist and friend, went all the way from Spennymoor to the Court. He drove all the way back because he knew I was very upset and, knowing me, guessed I'd want to go on stage to prove a point. I explained to the two owners of the club about my reservations about appearing and they said, "You must be joking and, whatever the outcome, if you can get back here tomorrow night, you do." This gave me confidence and I stood up in court on the following day like a man.

'On the way back to Spennymoor, Bert could see that I was upset and suggested we cut out part of the act, but as soon as I walked on to the stage to rapturous applause I walked over to Bert and said, "The lot." I'd cried on stage before, but before I'd finished that night the tears rolled down my cheeks because the audience knew that I'd been framed. Everybody in the audience stood up. Bert Gaunt came over and shook my hand. The next day the press came round and wrote an article headed, "Spennymoor saved my career." ' The case and verdict did not have any later adverse for the holiday season. 1962 had contained plenty of personal appearances, either as the Red Shadow or on the concert platform, but it was noticeable that there were no television or radio appearances. The next year was to see another change away from musical shows and on to overseas tours, a summer season at Blackpool and the usual Sunday concerts. David and his family and fans hoped for better things.

After the completion of the pantomime season at the beginning of 1963, David was booked for one of the tours he really enjoyed, a services tour. He visited Kenya, Aden and the Persian Gulf, where he renewed his acquaintance with the Royal Navy. It was at about this time that Bert Gaunt took over as David's musical director. They were both ex-Royal Navy so the partnership was almost bound to succeed, and with one or two minor hitches it did throughout the Sixties. He remembers David as: 'basically a kind man, with a great sense of humour. He was the most confident man I ever met, but he was also very stubborn. I remember I once suggested that he was singing too high and we needed to come down a note or two. He flatly refused so I brought the music down a little anyway and I don't think he really noticed. He could be a little wild, but when he seemed to be going really overboard I'd threaten to ring Shiela and he'd come back into line. Darts was his favourite after show pastime, he was very good, after years of practice, and he could almost will them into the spaces on the board. He was a lousy golfer, but again the ball wouldn't have dared to stay out of the hole.'

After the foreign tour, he found time to spend with his family in April,

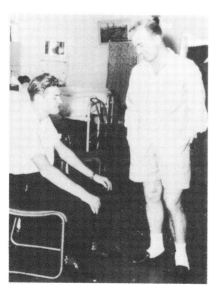

and they all flew off to the Canary Islands for the comparative luxury of a whole 16 days together. Yet another summer season in Blackpool followed and, during this stay, David managed to make a re-appearance on the radio in a show appropriately called *Blackpool Night*. The summer show in 1963 was named *The Five Star Show*. David, one of the 'stars', concentrated on singing light ballads. In fact the show was very musically inclined, his fellow

Talking to Guardsman Keith Arnison of Durham during a visit to the British Military Hospital, Nairobi, 1963
(*Picture courtesy* Hull Daily Mail)

99

effect in Spennymoor as they invited David straight back for their anniversary show the following year.

It was a great pity that a year that had started so well had finished in such a tragic way. David continued with his club performances with weekly stints at Liverpool, Paignton, Ilkeston and Consett but his appearance in the pantomime, *Robinson Crusoe,* at the Grand Theatre, Wolverhampton was cancelled, 'due to mutual agreement' according to the official hand-out. There can be little doubt that this cancellation was due to the court case a few months before. This was a definite low point in David's career and even his usual super-confidence had taken a dent.

Chapter Seventeen

The Wilderness Years (1967 to 1976)

During the eight years from 1967 to 1975 there was very little publicity of any kind for David, but this was by no means the end of his career as a performer. During these years the groups really held sway. Groups like the Beatles and the Rolling Stones, who became world performers and stars, far excelling anything that David had done in the Fifties. This is not to forget, however, that David could be considered as a trail-blazer leading the way for the many British singers who were to follow him to the U.S.A. during the Sixties and Seventies. It is noticeable that the 1979 *Guinness Book of British Hit Singles* has on its cover a picture of 24 performers who achieved big record hits over the years, and in the front row, wearing dark glasses, is David Whitfield. David's songs and style of singing were now considered 'square' among the teen-agers, but he still had a faithful following from his fans of the Fifties, now mothers of teenagers themselves.

Unfortunately, David's attraction towards younger women did not diminish over the years and this must have been a great source of worry for his family, but also for his agent and manager. One correspondent wrote about an incident concerning David when he appeared at Southsea in the Seventies: 'David always used to use the same café when he was appearing in Southsea. It wasn't far from the King's Theatre. The lady who owned the café always used to give David a warm welcome and, although it was a self-service café, they'd always wait on him. I was in the café in the late Seventies when a really scruffy looking bloke walked in with a young girl on his arm. He'd obviously had a few drinks and he called out for service, "What's up with you then, lost the use of your legs?" asked the café owner. "Don't you recognise me?", said the man and immediately opened his mouth, and the rich tones of *Cara Mia* filled the café. It was David, currently appearing at the Pier, an entirely different looking David, from the one who'd been the toast of Southsea, twenty years before.'

During the late Sixties and early Seventies clubs and restaurants were his main venues. The wheel had turned full circle from the huge crowded auditoriums of the provincial and London theatres to the intimate, smoky atmosphere of the working-men's clubs. He had the time in 1967 during a lull in his club engagements to take a holiday after his Easter week performance in Paignton. David, Shiela and the family journeyed to Jersey for a brief stay, the public traumas of the previous year almost forgotten.

He also turned much more to tours abroad. In 1967 he went to Australia and New Zealand during the English summer months, appearing in Sydney, Perth, Melbourne, Adelaide and Auckland. This was followed by a two-week Canadian tour in late October. Even though he seemed to have been forgotten, except for a still-loyal dwindling following of fans in the U.K and U.S.A., it seemed that there was still a rich potential for his style of singing in the Commonwealth countries. Lance, the eldest son, remembers the trip to Canada as one of his favourite memories of being with his father: 'In 1967, Dad took me with him to Canada where he was appearing at the Royal York Hotel in Toronto. I was 16 at the time and appeared with him on the Ed Sullivan Show. I remember Mr. Sullivan asking me all about the school system in England. I never did see the show on television, by the way. It was the first time I met Momma and Poppa, who on a previous visit had "adopted" Dad. We had a marvellous time and it was great to be with Dad on my own, so to speak.'

Apart from the trips abroad, this was a low period in David's life; he felt very disillusioned and let down by the record and show business concerns in Britain. The lack of work on stage, radio and television was partly his own fault. The court case of 1966 had not done him any favours. Any case concerning children was frowned on even more then than now. Nevertheless, he still had a hard core of devoted fans who flocked to his shows and performances at the end of the Sixties; not in the same volume as in the Fifties, but enough to gain him a reasonable billing in clubs and theatres. Above all, with all the faults in his personal life, he was a showman capable of filling a club or theatre with the sheer force of his personality alone. Added to this, he still had the very important asset of support from his family and close friends, and this must have helped carry him through his low periods.

In October, another morale booster was his return to the Variety and Sporting Club at Spennymoor for their anniversary show. He had been appearing there at the time of his court appearance in Wales, the year before, and it must have given him a huge fillip to be welcomed back again.

The following year, 1968, was his best year for theatre and club appearances since his heyday. He sang at many venues on the Northern circuit even appearing at the South Pier Theatre, Blackpool, where he received his usual large audiences and generous applause. He flew to Canada once again for a two-day television appearance in mid-January, and this was followed by a solid amount of bookings in the North and Midlands, until the beginning of April, when he returned to Toronto for a season at the Royal York Hotel.

Back in England for the summer, David appeared in club and seaside venues before returning to Canada, fast becoming his second home, for another tour at the end of September. It is noticeable that, although he had plenty of bookings, none of them were in London or the South. Even his old theatrical haunts in Portsmouth and Southsea seemed to have lost touch with him.

The next year, 1969, was the period when David spent more time abroad than in his home country, but even this trend was to be short-lived. The year started with two weeks in Toronto, followed by only six bookings in the next three months. He then had an Australian tour from May to July and then another six weeks in Canada beginning in August. It was obvious that he had to go where bookings were available, but it could not have improved his family life. The three Whitfield children were growing up fast, even the 'baby', Amanda Jane, was now ten, and they must have all missed their father during his trips across the Atlantic and to the other side of the world.

One other event of note happened in 1969: David made a rare appearance on television, appearing in the *Bernard Braden Show* on B.B.C.1, just before Christmas. As the host of the show was Canadian, it is probable that his popularity in Canada had the knock-on effect of enabling him to be booked for a British television show.

The early Seventies continued with the usual club appearances at home, interspersed with tours of Canada or Australia. In early 1970 there is no evidence of any bookings at all in the first two months, with only a solitary week in Scotland in March.

It seems that it was about this time also that the idea of leaving the U.K. and starting a new life in Australia first came to David, although it was several years later that the idea almost came to fruition. Bert Gaunt summed up the attraction of Australia for David when he said, 'It was a real man's country, macho in many ways; hard drinking and hard working, the sort of set-up that would really have appealed to him.'

There was other evidence in 1970 of a slump in the Whitfield family's fortunes. They moved from the grand *Cara Mia* house in Kirkella, David's pride and joy and in some ways, his status symbol, to a smaller house in Croft Drive, Anlaby. Still on the outskirts of the City of Hull but not quite so up-market. The days of a nanny to look after the children and teenage girls camping out on the adjoining grass verge were gone, never to return.

Lance has lots of memories of the days the family spent at *Cara Mia*:

'My bedroom was up in the attic, accessed by some pull-down steps. At one end of the room was a trap-door which went through to the attic proper. Grandpa (Mum's Dad) built a train set layout in there which went all the way round that part of the attic. There are many happy memories of having friends to stay up there. *Cara Mia* was a fabulous place, and I didn't realise when we left that I would miss it so much. There are vague memories of various stars like Des O'Connor being there.'

David's old contacts in Hull were still maintained and in 1970 any thoughts about emigration would have been partly stifled by his affection for his home town. An article in the *Hull Times* stated: 'Club proprietor Reg Williams did a little behind the scenes planning and brought two top Hull stars together to officially open the Northwood Club, Cottingham. David Whitfield, then in Stansted, Essex, found out about the starting of the club and asked if he could open it, giving his services free, for old times sake. Norman Collier did the same thing, and Reg agreed to both requests, making sure neither knew about the other.' Reg went on to talk about the club opening and his early memories of the young David Whitfield: 'When they both came along they were surprised to see each other. We had a great night, with Norman gagging and sabotaging David's attempts to sing. It was such a success that we repeated it the next night. I'd known the two stars from their early days in Hull's clubland, right back to David's courting days with Shiela.

I was an entertainer and once, when I was guesting at the Perth Street Club, David, then still in the Navy, asked if he could sing. He did sing and I thought that he, the volunteer, was ten times better than me, the guest artiste. We had a lot of laughs about that over the years.' Reg remained a good friend and confidant of David's throughout his life. It was the comradeship and support of this local club life that David missed in the hurly-burly of national and international showbusiness, although he was to fall out with his old friend, Norman Collier, in later years.

At the end of 1971, sadly, the final newsletter was issued from the David Whitfield Society. Until then a regular newsheet was posted to fans all over the country, but after this date, December 1971, fans had to write for information instead of automatically receiving it.

A glimpse of a week of David's bookings in March 1971 gives a good impression of the way his career had plummeted in Britain.

Sunday 21 March –   'Birdcage', Harlow.
Monday 22 March –   McVitie and Price, Harlesden.
Tuesday 23 March –   Eastleigh Barracks, Portsmouth.
Wednesday 24 March –   106 Club, Fareham.
Thursday 25 March –   W.M.C. Chatham.
Friday 26 March –   St. Mary's Club, Chadwell.
Saturday 27 March –   City Tradesman's Club, Welwyn Garden City.

Although the bookings did indicate that David was once again accepted in the South, it was a far cry from the London Palladium and the large southern seaside resort theatres.

Very little appears in the national and local press until 1974 when once again the only news was not really good publicity for him. *The Hull Daily Mail* of 9 February reported:

'David Whitfield X-rayed at Hull Royal Infirmary today – suspected rib injury caused by falling off the stage at a club in Lincoln Pavilion this week. Rib not cracked but chest was badly hurt. Shiela left for Swansea today where David is booked to appear at a club tomorrow night. He apparently slipped off a chair while singing *The Drinking Song.*' Quite an appropriate title, but this was probably another indication of his, by this time, serious drinking problems.

The first half of the 1970's were not the best years of the David Whitfield career. Bookings were scarce and he had really gone back to performances like his early club performances of the Forties. Anyone else would have probably been content to stick at that, but David's super optimism and confidence still came to the fore and, although he did not know at the time, the late Seventies were going to herald a new surge in his popularity at home and abroad with fresh opportunities 'Down-under'. He would have hated the idea, but, with his experience and unique way of handling an audience, he was already heading for the title of one of the elder statesmen of British song.

Chapter Eighteen

The Final Songs (1976-80)

The years from 1976 onwards were much better ones for David. It seemed that he had settled into a comfortable club routine around the British Isles with the occasional trip abroad, especially to Australia, where he was still a very firm favourite. His heavy drinking remained a problem: a glance at his photographs of the late-Seventies is an illustration of that.

He was represented by Carl Gresham Personal Management during this period and was billed as 'Britain's first cabaret attraction'. There was also a tendency to return to the theatre appearances that had been a bit short on the ground for the past few years. It looked as though David had turned the corner and was back on his way up. A return to good show business publicity also indicated a return to popularity, if not stardom.

Stage magazine reported in August: 'Negotiations with Jade for an early season show at the Wellington Pier, Great Yarmouth, had proved to be a success as they had included three stars who had been "till toppers" at past seasons' shows at the resort, David Whitfield, Yana and Stan Stennett. With the perky Monica Rose joining forces with them it will be quite a powerful line-up. As a romantic singer, David is still supreme. His fine, powerful voice really brought the best from a string of standards and ballads, such as *I Believe*. The applause was rapturous, for the audience wanted more.'

David did not actually complete the show, as he was confined to his bed with an unknown ailment for the last performance. He also missed the second of two night appearances at the Hull Hofbrauhaus, something he would never normally do in his home town.

Later, during the summer, a long hot one, David appeared at the Batley Variety Club, the self-styled 'showplace of the stars'. The local newspaper found the time and space to say: 'That idol of the Fifties, sentimental songster David Whitfield, really pulls them in.'

David was back in court again during 1976 when he had a slight confrontation with the Customs and Excise over his VAT. It appeared that during his tour of Australia in the previous year his company, David

Whitfield Enterprises Ltd., had failed to send in a VAT return and frequent requests for the return at later dates were ignored. Although David was found guilty and ordered to pay £50 with £25 costs, this fine was a lot less than the maximum which could have been £760. The blame was laid on the unfortunate company accountant, but, compared with some of the publicity in previous years, this was harmless. Public sympathy, in any case, involving the Customs and Excise or Inland Revenue, then as now, tended to be with the accused.

During the court case, David's mother had entered Castle Hill Hospital near Hull and he was visiting her during the proceedings. One of the accusations levelled at him, especially during his glory years, was that he did not bother to find time to visit his mother enough. This charge was probably aggravated by the fact that Shiela's parents spent a lot of time at the Whitfield house, usually in the capacity of unpaid baby-sitters during David's frequent trips abroad. It did, however, cause some ill-feeling between David and some of his family.

In November 1976 David appeared with many other stars at the City Varieties, Leeds. going on to tour clubs in the Manchester area for the rest of the month. Although he was making a re-appearance in theatre-land, with the slight upsurge in variety shows, he never returned to the days of Christmas pantomime. The Christmas season in 1976 was spent at the Poco Poco Club at Stockport, a far cry from the London Palladium and Victoria Palace of yesteryear.

The following year, 1977, marked his 25th year in show business. A lot had happened in those years. He had been to the heights of world stardom in the Fifties and then slumped towards the bottom in the late-Sixties and early Seventies. During this period he obviously had a lot to regret. The court case episodes and heavy drinking had taken their toll in his popularity and health, something no performer can really afford. Nevertheless, he was still reqired enough on the theatre and club circuit to earn a reasonable living, and, during all of those twenty-five years, he had brought a lot of happiness and enjoyment to many people. He still had the power to control an audience and he had kept his voice. His old friend Hughie Green remarked that, although drink and age had caught up with him at the end of the Seventies, David still had the power in his voice to fill a theatre without the assistance of the amplifiers and microphones so beloved of today's groups and entertainers.

The beginning of an article in the Dublin *Sunday World* at the end of 1977 appears to echo this sentiment: 'A rave from the grave is how some of the "in" pop punters describe David Whitfield today, with a fair amount of good reason. The silver-haired old fox has been around for more than a quarter of a century and he shows no sign of fading away.

'He looks a lot healthier than any of his younger ego-trippers battling for recognition on the Irish show business scene today. His voice sounds healthier too. And Whitfield can still walk out on to a stage and call the audience his own after ten minutes.'

Above all, during these later years David Whitfield remained a breath and reminder of the Fifties, unfashionable years, but years of comparative quiet where life and times seemed relatively un-complicated. When Friday night was dance night, the men wore jackets and ties and the music was still provided by the 'big' bands, usually with a lead singer or two.

1977 opened with the now usual round of club appearances, including ones at Solihull and Bradford. It was followed by a disappointment when a huge show due to take place in London, in February, was cancelled. The *London Evening News* wrote: 'Golden Stars to Shine Once More – the first concert featuring recording stars from the Fifties and Sixties is being organised at the Empire Pool, Wembley. An audience of 10,000 is expected. Helen Shapiro, Russ Conway, Bert Weedon, Ruby Murray, Frank Ifield, Acker Bilk and David Whitfield are due to appear. It is said that between these artists they were responsible for the sale of over 200 million records.' The show was cancelled before it got off the ground, hopefully not because of lack of public interest, but at least David's name was still there with the stars of previous years.

In the same month, February, David changed his agency once again when Mainline Entertainments took him on, with a personal manager called Terry McLeod. The change almost immediately bore fruit as David was booked for a summer season at the Opera House, Scarborough, in *Charlie's Music Hall*, with Charlie Williams.

A review about the show in *Stage* magazine in August read: 'Guest star David Whitfield started the season cold, a little un-used, perhaps, to presenting a theatre act after a lengthy spell working in cabaret; but he soon warmed to the more concise style and faster pace necessary, and by the end of the first week had the audiences shouting for more.' He obviously had not lost his touch!

Sundays were again taken over, as in the old days, this time with a series of evening shows at the Embassy Theatre, Skegness, called *The David Whitfield Show* and compèred by Kenneth Palmer.

In October, the *Daily Express* in cooperation with the *New Musical Express* published the all-time champions of the record charts. The system was a simple one, 30 points were awarded each week to the number one record, 29 points for second place, with a sliding scale to one point for thirtieth place. Although this was based on hit parade performance rather than sales, it was a useful and reliable indicator to those artistes with most staying power. It is worth noting that David finished, at the time, above such artistes as Connie Francis, Tom Jones, The Hollies, The Supremes, Shirley Bassey and Nat King Cole. Out of 30 performers, David was listed twelfth, the title being won by – Elvis Presley.

Presentation of a radio microphone at the Royal Opera House, Scarborough, 1977, to commemorate David's 25 years in show business

The good publicity continued to the end of the year, not only in the local press but nationally as well. The *Daily Mail* published an article in December entitled *All Time Top Ten,* and among the artistes mentioned was David Whitfield with *Cara Mia*, and a reminder that it was Number One for ten weeks.

His 25th anniversary was not to be allowed to go by un-noticed by his fans, and a national daily reported; 'Still going strong – the golden boy of the Fifties. David Whitfield, who rose to popularity with light ballads in the Fifties, is back at Wolverhampton's Grand Theatre in a music hall revival. Hearts and soul singer David Whitfield could belong to the Fifties. But as he proves on stage this week, he is no back number. The hair is a little thinner, whitish gold, the complexion tanned by regular trips to Australia and New Zealand. Otherwise it's the same David Whitfield who charmed millions in the Fifties when he was the first British singer to get in the American hit parade and the first to get a golden disc.

'A few weeks ago fans from the Midlands and other parts of the country travelled to Scarborough to take him by surprise. He said he did not realise he had been in show business for 25 years. They knew to the day and marked the occasion after the show by presenting him with a radio microphone and a wrist watch.'

So David had returned to variety and popular ballads. He had returned to the old songs and away from light operetta, and the audiences were coming back. Perhaps he should never have moved away from the pops in the first place? One of his many fans gives the other point of view when she writes: 'I think David became a popular singer too late, because by the late Fifties rock and roll had come along and it was the beginning of the end of David's great popularity. If he'd become a famous singer in the Thirties or Forties, I'm sure he would have been in many musical comedies and light operettas and could have made films. I recently watched a Nelson Eddy and Jeanette McDonald film and she had a beautiful voice, but I didn't think much of him. David would have been far better in my opinion.'

The final years of the Seventies were marked by more and more trips to Australia and Canada, and the idea was definitely forming in David's mind about the prospect of starting a new life and career in the Antipodes.

Some things, however, could not be hidden even in Australia. A correspondent, who lived in Hull and knew David in his early club days in England stated: 'Some years ago, in the late Seventies I think, my wife

Still in full song

and I went to see him (David) do a show at the Epping R.S.L. Club, in a suburb of Sydney. From memory I think it could only have been a couple of years before he died in Sydney.

'Before the show we got chatting in the bar about Hull and our navy days, and I must admit that I was rather saddened by David's appearance. His hair was dyed a dreadful yellow colour and even before the show commenced he was visibly affected by alcohol. Indeed as the show progressed both my wife and I cringed with embarrassment for him. He gave the audience a few snatches of his magnificent voice interspersed with a lot of tomfoolery.

'Those in the audience who knew what a gifted singer he was, and those who had never heard of him were equally disappointed. Through the years since my wife (who also hails from Hull) and I have recalled that evening with sorrow. What had brought him to this?'

So what did bring him to this? Like nearly all stage performers he needed to be liked and admired. If they are fortunate enough to reach the top of the ladder in show business, and David certainly did, they obviously find it very difficult on the way down. Some performers have two personalities and lives, one for the public, and one personal, private one. It is probably true that David Whitfield had great difficulty in distinguishing one from the other, and, although he always said that he enjoyed returning home to Hull where he felt he could be himself, in reality it was alcohol and the adulation of young fans that really gave him that feeling of reassurance. Perhaps coming from a humble background as he did, he could handle the rise to stardom, he had something to prove. But the subsequent decline was harder to deal with.

The words of a fellow entertainer of the Fifties gives a good summing up of David Whitfield, and it would probably have been exactly the same if he had remained as a concrete mixer; 'David as a person? The tone in his voice really explains him. Gusty, macho, very confident, almost to the point of arrogance. Couldn't give a damm about anything really. Kept the teenage hunger for life and fun, wine, woman and song all his life. Women got him into hot water, especially the young ones, and I think wine finally killed him.'

David died in the Royal North Shore Hospital, Sydney, Australia on 15 February, 1980, just before his 54th birthday. He died of a cerebral haemorrhage after being taken to the intensive care unit of the hospital. He went into a deep coma soon after admittance and died within two hours. An account in the Australian *Daily Telegraph* reported: 'Whitfield, a former cement worker from Hull, had an alluring stage charm that made a him a favourite with women. His Australian promoter and long-time friend, Mr. Gordon White, said yesterday, "David and I took a 14-day sea cruise following the club tour and he seemed in very good health. Then, on Monday night he took a turn and was rushed to hospital.

"This was his thirteenth visit to Australia and he has always been an immense success here. His body will be cremated at Northern Suburbs Cemetery at 11.40 tomorrow and then I will fly his ashes home to his wife Shiela." '

So, just when it seemed that David was finding a new rôle for himself in show business, it all came to an abrupt halt. He died as he had lived, on tour entertaining, which is the end he would have chosen.

Fourteen years on, he is still not forgotten, especially amongst the 50-plus age group. His records are still played on radio programmes, sometimes by disc jockeys who were not born when he was a top recording star. His faithful band of fans, male and female, in the two Societies at either end of the country, work hard to keep his name alive and to raise money for charity.

Love him, or hate him, there can be little doubt that he forced his name into the record books of pop music by sheer determination and force of personality. He was a man of the Fifties who is still remembered by the older generation the length and breadth of the country and possibly overseas as well. Try mentioning the song *Cara Mia* to anyone who is over the age of 50. The reply will always come back – David Whitfield.

David sitting beside the pool at his Australian residence with Gordon White in the water, 1980. The last photograph of David, taken only four hours before the onset of the illness which ended in his death

DAVID WHITFIELD TOUR DATES TAKEN FROM
THE FAN CLUB MAGAZINE
FROM ME TO YOU
1957-1971

1957

October	*Royal Command Performance*	London Palladium
December 23rd (for a season)	LONDON, Palladium	*Robinson Crusoe*

1958

Spring	SOUTHSEA	
	DERBY	
June 28th-October 11th	BLACKPOOL, Opera House	*Big Show of 1958*
(for a season)		
Sat 24th May	*Dave King Show*	ITV Network
Monday 27th October (6 wks)	COVENTRY, Theatre	*The Birthday Show*
Wednesday 24th December	BIRMINGHAM, Hippodrome	*Robinson Crusoe*
(for a season)		

1959

April	MANCHESTER	
	LIVERPOOL	
July 2nd (10 wks)	BOURNEMOUTH, Pavilion	*The Big Show of 1959*
(for a season)		
June 20th	*Summer Spectacular*	ITV Network
July 19th, August 9th,	BLACKPOOL, Opera House	Sunday Concerts
August 30th, September 20th		
September 21st (1 week)	HULL, Regal	
October 10th	*Sunday Night at the London Palladium*	ITV Network
December (for a season)	BRIGHTON, Palladium	*Humpty Dumpty*

1960

March (for a season)	Australian Tour	
August 22nd	LONDON, Victoria Palace	*Rose Marie*
Dec 20th – Jan 21st	EDINBURGH	
Sunday Concerts		
Aug 7th	BLACKPOOL, Opera House	
Aug 14th	BRIDLINGTON, Spa Royal	
Aug 21st	MORECAMBE, Winter Gardens	
Sept 11th	BLACKPOOL, Winter Gardens	
Sept 18th	BLACKPOOL, Opera House	
Oct 9th	LEICESTER, De Montfort Hall	
Nov 13th	DONCASTER	
Nov 20th	PETERBOROUGH	
Nov 27th	HULL	

1961

Jan 23rd – Feb 18th	GLASGOW	*Rose Marie* (Tour)
Feb 20th – Feb 25th	HULL	
Feb 27th – Mar 11th	NEWCASTLE	
Mar 13th – Mar 25th	COVENTRY	
Mar 27th – Apr 15th	MANCHESTER	
Apr 17th – May 6th	LIVERPOOL	
May 8th – May 27th	BIRMINGHAM	

May 29th – Jun 3rd	NOTTINGHAM	*Rose Marie* (Tour)
Sunday Concerts		
Feb 5th	CARLISLE, Lonsdale Theatre	
March 5th	*Sunday Night at the London Palladium*	ITV Network
April 30th	BRADFORD, Gaumont	
May 14th	GLOUCESTER, Regal	
May 21st	PORTSMOUTH, Guildhall	
July 16th, Aug 13th	MORECAMBE, Winter Gardens	
Aug 20th	SCARBOROUGH, Floral Hall	
July 23rd	*Blackpool Night*	BBC Light Programme
July 5th (season)	BLACKPOOL, Hippodrome	*Rose Marie*
Oct 9th (2wks)	BRIGHTON	*Rose Marie*
Nov 20th	BRISTOL	*Rose Marie*
Dec (season)	LEEDS, Grand	*Sleeping Beauty*

1962

Apr 17th – May 5th	*The Desert Song*	
	NOTTINGHAM, Theatre Royal	
May 7th – May 26th	BIRMINGHAM, Hippodrome	
May 28th Jun 23rd	LIVERPOOL, Empire	
Jun 25th Jul 21st	MANCHESTER, Palace	
Jul 23rd – Aug 11th	BRISTOL, Hippodrome	
Aug 13th – Sept 1st	COVENTRY, Theatre	
Sept 3rd – Sept 33nd	NEWCASTLE, Empire	
Sept 24th – Oct 13th	GLASGOW, Empire	
Oct 16th – Oct 20th	HULL, ABC	
Oct 22nd – Nov 10th	LEEDS, Grand	
Nov 12th – Nov 24th	SHEFFIELD, Lyceum	
Sunday Concerts		
June 17th	DOUGLAS I.O.M., Villa Marina	
July 8th	MORECAMBE, Winter Gardens	
July 15th	SCARBOROUGH, Floral Hall	
July 29th	TORQUAY, Princess	
Aug 19th	GT. YARMOUTH, Wellington Pier	
Aug 26th	MARGATE, Winter Gardens	
Sept 2nd	MORECAMBE, Winter Gardens	
Sept 16th	BLACKPOOL, Opera House	
Oct 7th	BLACKPOOL, Opera House	
Winter Season	LIVERPOOL, Empire	*Sleeping Beauty*

1963

Winter Season till 23rd Feb	LIVERPOOL, Empire	*Sleeping Beauty*
14th Mar – 7th Apr	Kenya, Aden & Persian Gulf	Services Tour
11th Apr – 27th Apr	Holiday with family	Canary Islands
22nd Jun – 5th Oct	BLACKPOOL, Winter Gardens	
(for a season)		
July 9th	B.B.C. Radio	*Blackpool Night*
Sunday Concerts		
July 7th	DOUGLAS I.O.M.	Villa Marina
July 14th	BRIDLINGTON	Spa
July 28th	MORECAMBE	Winter Gardens
Aug 11th	DOUGLAS I.O.M.	Villa Marina
Sept 1st	SCARBOROUGH	Floral Hall
Sept 15th	LLANDUDNO	Pier Pavilion
Dec 24th - March 14th	SHEFFIELD, Lyceum	*Goldilocks and 3 Bears*
(for a season)		

1964

Up to March 14th	SHEFFIELD, Lyceum	*Goldilocks and Three Bears*
	Holiday with family	Holland
April 16th	Singapore and Malaya	Services Tour
May 18th	SCARBOROUGH, Floral Hall	
June 19th – Sept 19th		
(for a season)	GREAT YARMOUTH, Britannia	*All in Favour*
Oct 15th	JOHANNESBURG/CAPETOWN	Services Tour
No Sunday Concerts		
Dec 22nd – Feb 20th	LEEDS, Grand	*Goldilocks and Three Bears*
(for a season)		

1965

Up to Feb 20th	LEEDS, Grand	*Goldilocks and Three Bears*
Various Clubs including:	WIGAN	
	BOLTON	
	BRADFORD, Talk of Yorkshire	
	OLLERTON, Miners Welfare Club	
	ROTHERHAM, Greasborough Social	
	WAKEFIELD, Theatre Club	
March 29th (week)	WOLVERHAMPTON, Grand Theatre	
Easter Sunday	BRIDLINGTON	
April 25th (week)	North East Tour including:	
	STOCKTON	
	MIDDLESBROUGH	
	SOUTH SHIELDS, La Strada	
May 2nd (week)	NEWCASTLE, La Dolce Vita	
July 3rd – Sept 11th	MORECAMBE, Winter Gardens *Summer Spectacular*	
(for a season)		
Sept 19th	*The Anniversary Show*	ITV Network
June 6th	SCARBOROUGH, Floral Hall	
July 4th	LLANDUDNO, Pier Pavilion	
July 11th	DOUGLAS, I.O.M., Villa Marina	
Aug 15th	DOUGLAS, I.O.M., Villa Marina	
Aug 22nd	LLANDUDNO, Pier Pavilion	
Sept 19th	*Sunday Night at the London Palladium*	ITV Network
Sept 20th (week)	SCARBOROUGH, Floral Hall	
Oct 10th (week)	WAKEFIELD, Kon-Tiki Club	
Oct 24th (week)	SOUTH SHIELDS, SUNDERLAND, La Strada Clubs	
Oct 31st (week)	WIGAN, BOLTON	
Nov 7th (week)	DONCASTER, Scala Progressive Club	
Nov 21st (week)	LEIGH, Garrick Theatre Club	
	WARRINGTON, Towers Club	
Nov 28th (week)	MIDDLESBROUGH, Marimba Club	
	DARLINGTON,La Bamba Club	
Dec 5th (week)	SOUTHPORT, Kingsway Club	
Dec 13th (week)	WORKSOP, Ace of Clubs	
	CHESTERFIELD	

1966

Jan-May	BLACKBURN
(exact dates unknown)	LEEDS
	BURNLEY
	WIDNES
	OLLERTON
	ROTHERHAM
	WIGAN
	BOLTON
May 11th (week)	ECCLES, Talk of the North
May 15th (week)	BRIGHOUSE, Ritz Casino Club
May 22nd (week)	CARDIFF, Cleopatra Club
June 12th (week)	SUNDERLAND
	SOUTH SHIELDS, La Strada Clubs
July 4th-Sept 10th	LLANDUDNO, Pier Pavilion *Gaytime*
(for a season)	
Sunday Concerts	
May 29th	BRIDLINGTON, Spa Royal Hall
June 26th	LLANDUDNO, Pier Pavilion
Aug 7th	SCARBOROUGH, Floral Hall
Sept 25th (week)	LEEDS, Seacroft Bowl
Oct 9th (week)	SPENNYMOOR, Variety and Sporting Club
Oct 31st (week)	LIVERPOOL, Shakespeare Club
Nov 7th (week)	PAIGNTON, Manor Club
Oct 26th (only)	ILKESTON, Albion Restaurant and Derby Regency Suite
Oct 30th (only)	LIVERPOOL, Litherland Club
Dec 18th (week)	CONSETT, Consett Bowl

David should have been appearing in *Robinson Crusoe* at the Grand Theatre, Wolverhampton, but this was cancelled due to mutual agreement.

1967

Jan 8th (week)	CASTLEFORD, Castleford Club
Jan 15th (week)	SOUTHPORT, Kingsway
Exact dates unknown	STOCKTON
	DONCASTER
	YORK
	LEEDS
	WAKEFIELD
	BIRMINGHAM
Easter (week)	PAIGNTON
	Holiday with family to Jersey
June-Sept	*Australian/N.Z. Tour* calling at:
	SYDNEY, St. George's League Club
	PERTH
	MELBOURNE
	ADELAIDE, Freeway Hotel
	AUCKLAND, Town Hall *Startime '67*
Oct 8th (week)	SPENNYMOOR, Variety and Sporting Club
Oct 17th (2 weeks)	*Canadian Tour*
Nov (week)	SOLIHULL
	HUCKNALL
Dec 17th (week)	YORK, De Grey Rooms

1968

Jan 7th	BIRMINGHAM, Castaways Club
Jan16th/17th	*Canadian TV Appearances*
Jan-March	BURNLEY
Club circuit/Theatres	BLACKBURN
Exact dates unknown	SWANSEA
	BEDLINGTON
	CONSETT
	SPENNYMOOR
	MIDDLESBROUGH
	BIRMINGHAM
	MANCHESTER
	BATLEY, Variety Club
	BLACKPOOL, South Pier Theatre
	PRESTON
	WAKEFIELD, Theatre Club
	DONCASTER
April 6th	TORONTO (Canada), Royal York Hotel
July 21st (week)	BRIGHOUSE, Ritz Casino Club
July 28th (week)	LIVERPOOL, Litherland Social Club
Aug 4th (week)	ROTHERAM, Greasborough Social Club
Aug 25th (only)	BRIDLINGTON, Grand Pavilion
Sept 22nd (only)	BLACKPOOL, A.B.C. Theatre
End September	*Canadian Tour*
Nov 24th	BRIGHOUSE, Ritz Casino Club
Nov ?	PUDSEY, West End Social Club
	MANCHESTER, Golden Garter Club
	LEEDS, Ace of Clubs
Dec 22nd (2 weeks)	WAKEFIELD, Theatre Club

1969

Jan 13th (2 weeks)	TORONTO, Royal York Hotel	
Jan – May	BIRMINGHAM	
(exact dates not known)	BOLTON	
	CHESTER	
	HULL	
	SUNDERLAND	
	GLASGOW	
May – July	AUSTRALIAN TOUR	
Aug (6 weeks)	CANADIAN TOUR	
Oct	BIRMINGHAM Area	
Dec 5th	WOLVERHAMPTON, Civic Hall	
Dec 20th	*Bernard Braden Show*	B.B.C. 1

1970

March 2nd (week)	EAST KILBRIDE
April 7th to April 20th	HALIFAX (Nova Scotia) Canadian Tour
April 26th (week)	GLOUCESTER, Whitcombe Lodge Club
	LONDON

Whitsuntide	DUNDEE, Whitehall Theatre
May (week)	LIVERPOOL
End July	CARDIFF
Aug 10th (week)	WAKEFIELD, Theatre Club
Aug 17th (week)	IRELAND
Aug 23rd	LEIGH, Carrick Theatre Club
Oct	CANADIAN TOUR
Nov	MORECAMBE, Bowl
	GARSTANG

1971

Jan – March	HONG KONG TOUR
April – Nov	AUSTRALIAN TOUR
Sun 21st March	HARLOW, Birdcage
Mon 22nd March	HARLESDEN, McVitie & Price
Tue 23rd March	PORTSMOUTH, Eastleigh Barracks
Wed 24th March	FAREHAM, 106 Club
Thu 25th March	CHATHAM, W.M.C.
Fri 26th March	CHADWELL, St. Mary's Club
Sat 27th March	WELWYN GARDEN CITY, City Tradesmen's Club

After this information (December 1971 Newsletter) the David Whitfield Society was virtually closed as one had to write in for information instead of receiving a newsheet.

RECORDING SESSIONS

Title	Composer	Publisher	Accompaniment	Date
I'll never forget you		Lennox	N. Temple	1/53
Marta	Simons; Gilbert	L. Wright	N. Temple	1/53
I Believe	Drake; Shirl; Graham; Stillman	Cromwell Music Inc.	Johnny Douglas	3/53
I'll make you mine		Pickwick	Johnny Douglas	3/53
The bridge of sighs	Reid	P. Maurice/KPM	Johnny Douglas	3/53
I'm the King of broken hearts		C. & C.	Roland Shaw	5/53
Answer me my love	Sigman; Winkler; Rauch	Gema/Bourne M.	Stanley Black	
Dance gypsy dance		S.Bron	Stanley Black	
Rags to riches		Chappell	Stanley Black	
Mardi Gras		Robbings	Stanley Black	
Laugh		Chappell	Stanley Black	
The Book	Gotwald; Roberts	Kassner	Stanley Black	1/54
Heartless		Lennox	Stanley Black	1/54
It's never too late to pray	Allen; Andre Machen	M. Reine Music	Stanley Black	5/54
Cara Mia	Trapani; Lange	Leo Feist	Mantovani	5/54
How, when or where	Reine; May	M. Reine Music	Mantovani	5/54
Love tears and kisses		Vic.	Mantovani	5/54
Smile (Theme from Modern Times)	Chaplin; Turner; Parsons	Bourne Music	Eric Rogers	7/54
Santo Natale (Merry Christmas		Memory Lane M.	Stanley Black	10/54
Adeste Fideles (Come all ye faithful)			Stanley Black	10/54
Open your heart		Chappell	Mantovani	1/55
Beyond the stars	Trapani; Lange	Robbins Music	Mantovani	1/55
Mama		P. Maurice	R. Shaw Orch.	4/55
Ev'rywhere		S. Bron	R. Shaw Orch.	4/55
Lady of Madrid		Southern	R. Shaw Orch.	3/55
I'll never stop loving you	Cahn; Brodszky	Robbins	R. Shaw Orch.	3/55
Santa Rosa Lea Rose		Burlington	R. Shaw Orch.	6/55
The Lady		L. Spier	R. Shaw Orch.	6/55
Angelus		Robbins	Mantovani	9/55
When you lose the one you love	Pelosi; Arden; Harper	B. Wood	Mantovani and Chorus	9/55
The Rudder and the Rock	Oliver; Glaser; Warren; McGehen	L. Spier	R. Shaw Orch.	12/55
My September love	Evans	Hit Songs	R. Shaw Orch.	12/55
My son John	Fain; Leigh	Anglo Pic Music	R. Shaw Orch.	3/56
My unfinished symphony		J. Fields	R. Shaw Orch.	3/56
If I lost you		Robbins	R. Shaw Orch.	10/56
The Adoration Waltz	Stock; Lewis	S. Bron	R. Shaw Orch.	10/56
It's almost tomorrow			Mac Melodies	5/56
Martinella		Wigmore & Anglo Con.	R. Shaw Orch.	1/57
I'll find you (from the film Sea Wife) Robbins				1/57
I'll find you (shortened version for film use only)				1/57
I'd give you the world			Mac Melodies	1/57
Ev'rything		Bron.	R. Shaw Orch.	1/57
Without him		Joy Music	R. Shaw Orch.	3/57
Dream of Paradise			Henderson	3/57
Maria (from West Side Story)	Bernstein; Sondheim	Chappell, G. Schirmer	Orch: Con. P. Conrad	10/57

Title	Writers	Publisher	Orch/Conductor	Date
My one true love		Robbins	Orch: Con. P. Conrad	10/57
Maria				12/57
Cry my heart	Berry		Mantovani	1/58
My one true love	Robbins		Mantovani	1/58
On the street where you live (from *My Fair Lady*)	Loewe; Lerner		Chappell	2/58
Afraid	Evans; Mullen		S. Bron	3/58
William Tell	Shaw; Purcell	Robbins	Roland Shaw	3&4/58
Poppa Piccolino	Mascheroni; Musel	Chappell, Britico	R. Shaw Orch. Cond. by Paul Conrad	1/58
Intro: Funiculi Funicula	Denza	B.I.E.M.	,,	2/58
Lover come back to me	Romberg; Hammerstein II	Chappell	,,	3/58
Unless	Evans; Hargreaves; Damerell	F.D.&H.	,,	3/58
Song of the Vagabonds	Friml; Hooker	Feldman	,,	3/58
My one true love	Conrad; Whitfield	Robbins	,,	3/58
Only a Rose	Friml; Hooker	Feldman	,,	3/58
Vienna City of my dreams	Sieczynski	A. H. & Crew	,,	3/58
March of the Grenadiers	Scherzinger; Grey; Connelly	C. Connelly	,,	3/58
The Desert Song	Romberg; Harbach; Hammerstein	Chappell	,,	3/58
Throw open wide your window	May; Stanley	Chas Brull	,,	3/58
Tell me tonight	Spoliansky; Eyton	Chappell/M.C.P.S.	,,	3/58
Good-Bye	Stolz; Reisch; Graham	Chappell	,,	3/58
The Right to love	Wolf; Raleigh	B. Wood	Roland Shaw	6/58
That's when your heartaches begin	Fisher; Raskin	Robbins		6/58
The White Dove	Grey; Lehar	Chappell	Roland Shaw	10/58
Serenade from *The Student Prince*	Romberg; Donnelly	Chappell	Roland Shaw	10/58
Love is a stranger	Conrad; Whitfield	Robbins	Roland Shaw	10/58
This is Lucia	Wizell; Losbona	Yale	Roland Shaw	10/58
Farewell my love	Conrad	B. Wood	Roland Shaw	12/58
Willingly	Giraud; Sigman; Broussolle	Macmelodies KPM/Britico	R. Shaw Orch.	12/58
A Million Stars	Reid	Cine		6/59
When your hair has turned to silver		Cam.Conn.		6/59
Silver hair and heart of gold		P. Maurice		6/59
That old fashioned mother of mine		L. Wright		6/59
I'm in the mood for love		Robbins		6/59
Trust in me		L. Wright		6/59
When I grow too old to dream		Robbins		6/59
Oh Tree	Reid	Merit	Roland Shaw	9/59
Our love waltz	Conrad	B. Wood	Roland Shaw	9/59
Climb every mountain (*The Sound of Music*)	Rogers; Hammerstein	Williamson	Roland Shaw	12/59
The Sound of Music	Rogers; Hammerstein	Williamson	Roland Shaw	12/59
Song of the dreamer	Stock	S. Bron	Roland Shaw	12/59

My only love	Stanford; Newell; Humphries	F.D.&H.	Roland Shaw	12/59
Angela Mia (Ti Adoro) (My Angel from Heaven) U.S.A. version	Conrad	Robbins	Roland Shaw	12/59
A Tear, A Kiss, A Smile	Insetta; Gilbert	L. Spier	R. Shaw Orch.	2/60
My Heart and I (from *Old Chelsea*)	Tauber; Tysh	L. Wright	Acc:Dir.R.Shaw	2/60
I kiss your hand, Madame (from *Old Chelsea*)	Erwin; Lewis; Rotter,	Chappell	Acc:Dir.R.Shaw	2/60
O, Maiden, my maiden (from *Frederica*)	Lehar; Pepper	Chappell	Acc:Dir.R.Shaw	2/60
Gipsy moon (from *Frederica*)	Borgandff; Eyton	Chappell	Acc:Dir.R.Shaw	2/60
Your eyes (from *White Horse Inn*)	Stolz; Benatzky; Graham	Chappell	Acc:Dir.R.Shaw	2/60
Serenade (from *The Student Prince*)	Donnelly; Romberg	Chappell	Acc:Dir.R.Shaw	10/58
You are my heart's delight (from *The Land of Smiles*)	Lehar; Smith; Graham	Chappell		2/60
Gold and Silver	Lehar; Park	Blocken-Vorlag	Acc:Dir.R.Shaw	2/10
If I am Dreaming (from *The Dubarry*)	Millocker; MacKenben; Leigh	Chappell	Acc:Dir.R.Shaw	2/60
The Blue Danube (from *The Dubarry*)	Strauss; Dunn	Feldman	Acc:Dir.R.Shaw	2/60
You, just you (from *Wild Violets*)	Stolz; Carter	Chappell	Acc:Dir.R.Shaw	2/60
The white dove (from *The Rogue Song*)			Acc:Dir.R.Shaw	2/60
Hear my song, Violetta	Klose; Lukesch; Pepper	Brittico/Dix Ltd.	Acc:Dir. Paul Conrad	10/60
I Believe	Drake; Shirl; Graham; Stillman	Cinephonic, Crom Mus. BMI	Acc:Dir. Paul Conrad	10/60
Ramona	Wayne; Gilbert	F.D.& H.	Paul Conrad and his Orch.	11/60
Alone	Freed; Brown	Big 3 Music	,,	11/60
Look for the Silver Lining	Kern; De Sylva	Chappell	,,	11/60
You'll never walk alone	Rodgers; Hammerstein II	Williamson	,,	11/60
Trees	Kilmer; Rasbach	Chappell	,,	11/60
Wonderful One	Whiteman; Grofe; Neilan; Terriss	F.D.& H.	,,	11/60
Love's Last Word is Spoken	Bixio; Sievier	Ascherberg, BIEN, Hopwood, Crewe	,,	11/60
You are too beautiful	Rodgers; Hart	Chappell	,,	12/60
Can I forget you	Kern; Hammerstein	Chappell	,,	12/60
Devotion	Cesana	Kassner	,,	12/60
My Moonlight Madonna	Fioich; Scotti; Webster	K. Prowse	,,	11/60
Song of the Mounties	Friml;Harbach;Hammerstein	Chappell	,,	
Why shouldn't we (with Janet Waters)	Friml;Harbach;Hammerstein	Chappell	,,	
Rose Marie (with Janet Waters)	Friml;Harbach;Hammerstein; Webster	Chappell	,,	
Right place for a girl (with Janet Waters)	Friml;Harbach;Hammerstein; Webster	Chappell	,,	

Indian Love Call (with Janet Waters)	Friml; Harbach; Hammerstein; Webster	Chappell	,,	11/60
I have the love			*Never released*	9/60
A Scottish Soldier	Stewart; Arr. MacFadyen	J. S. Kerr		2/61
Scotland the Brave	Trad.	Burlington		2/61
Blue Heaven (from *The Desert Song*) (with Janet Waters)			Choir & Orch. Con. P. Conrad	12/60
I want a kiss (with Janet Waters)				11/60
One alone				11/60
The Riff song				12/60
One flower in your garden				12/60
French Military Marching Song				12/60
Cara Mia	Trapani; Lange	Robbins Music	Roland Shaw and his Orch.	
Who can I turn to (When Nobody Needs Me) (from *The Roar of the Greasepaint, the Smell of the Crowd*)	Bricusse; Newley	Concorde	,,	
On a clear day you can see forever	Lane; Lerner		,,	
If ever I would leave you (from *Camelot*)	Loewe; Lerner	Chappell	,,	
A man without love	Callander; Ornadel			
Mama	Bixio; Parsons; Turner; Cherubin	Mac Melodies/ B.I.E.M.	,,	
Because you're mine	Cahn; Brodszky		,,	
Stranger in Paradise (from *Kismet*)	Wright; Forrest; Blanche	Frank Music	,,	
If I ruled the world	Ornadel; Bricusse		,,	
Softly as I leave you	De Vita; Calabrese; Shaper		,,	
Because	D'Hardelot; Teschemacher		,,	
What kind of fool am I	Bricusse; Newley		,,	
I can't stop loving you	Gibson	Acuff-Rose	,,	8/66
I will know	Spearing	Palace Music	,,	8/66
If you love me (I won't care)	Monnot; Parsons; Piaf	P. Morris/KPM/ Britico	,,	8/66

TOP THIRTY HIT RECORDS

Many of David Whitfield's records entered the Top Thirty lists and set out below are the dates and the positions that David's records reached from 1953 to 1960.

1953	*Oct*	*2*			
Bridge of Sighs		9th for 1 week			
	Oct	*16*			
Answer Me		1st, in the the charts for 13 weeks			
	Dec	*11*			
Rags to Riches		3rd, for 1 week			

1954	*Jan*	*8*			
Rags to Riches		3rd, in charts for 10 weeks			
	Jan	*29*			
Answer Me		12th for I week			
	Mar	*19*			
The Book		5th, in charts for 12 weeks			
	May	*28*			
The Book		10th, in charts for 3 weeks			
	June	*18*			
Cara Mia		1st, in charts for 25 weeks			
	Nov	*12*			
Santo Natale		2nd, in charts for 10 weeks			

1955	*Feb*	*5*	*12*	*19*	*26*
Beyond the Stars		11th	9th	5th	8th
	Jul	*2*	*23*		
Mama		13th	10th		
	Aug	*13*	*20*	*27*	
Ev'rywhere		7th	4th	4th	
	Sept	*3*	*10*	*17*	*24*
		4th	4th	4th	4th
	Oct	*1*	*8*	*15*	*22*	*29*
		5th	4th	6th	10th	10th

	Nov	*5*	*12*	*26*	
		14th	17th	15th	
When You Lose the One You Love	*Dec* 21st	*3* 12th	*10* 14th	*17* 15th	*24*
1956 When You Lose the One You Love	*Jan* 14th	*7* 13th	*14* 10th	*21* 10th	*28*
	Feb	*4* 8th	*11* 15th		
My September Love	*Mar*	*3* 23rd	*10* 20th	*24* 18th	*31* 19th
Rudder and the Rock	*Mar*	*3* 24th	*17* 19th		
My September Love	*Apr*	*7* 17th	*14* 12th	*21* 9th	*28* 8th
	May	*5* 7th	*12* 4th	*19* 5th	*26* 4th
	Jun	*2* 5th	*9* 7th	*16* 8th	*23* 8th	*30* 9th
	Jul	*7* 11th	*14* 15th		
1956 My Son John	*Aug*	*4* 26th	*25* 18th		
	Sep	*1* 13th			
1957 Adoration Waltz	*Jan*	*3* 33rd	*26* 16th		
	Feb	*2* 15th	*9* 16th	*16* 20th	*23* 17th
	Mar	*2* 11th	*9* 12th	*16* 14th	*23* 16th

1958
On The Street Where You Live

	May	3	17	24
		27th	19th	18th

	Jun	7	21
		28th	18th

	Jul	5	12	19	26
		18th	19th	19th	19th

	Aug	8
The Right to Love

30th for 1 week

1960
I Believe

Nov *24*
49th for 1 week
(This was the last David Whitfield record to
appear in the Top Fifty of the Hit Parade)